The **WEI-CHUAN COOKING SCHOOL** was founded in 1961 as a subsidiary of the Wei-Chuan Food Corporation, the largest food supplier in Taiwan. The school quickly became the largest and most respected institution of its kind along the Asia-Pacific rim. Graduates include world-class chefs, institutional teachers, professional caterers, connoisseurs of Chinese and international cuisine, as well as many dedicated homemakers.

As the school's reputation grew, requests came from all over the world for guidance and information about recipes offered in the cooking classes. To meet this demand, "Chinese Cuisine" was published in 1972. It was an immediate hit and led to a continued succession of popular Wei-Chuan Publishing cookbooks.

Wei-Chuan Publishing, long recognized for producing the most authentic and comprehensive Asian cuisine cookbooks has now expanded its horizons to include popular cuisine from around the world. For nearly thirty years, Wei-Chuan's signature bilingual Chinese/English cookbooks have ensured that more readers around the world may enjoy its cookbooks.

Wei-Chuan's success can be attributed to its commitment to providing the best quality product possible. All recipes are complemented by full color photographs and each recipe is written with easy-to-follow instructions and precisely measured ingredients. Wei-Chuan's mission is to share its recipes with those who value the pleasures of cooking and eating.

異國風味

南洋菜
星加坡 馬來西亞 印尼

Singaporean, Malaysian & Indonesian Cuisine

謝如意 Christina Sjahir Hwang

味全食譜
Wei-Chuan Cookbook

作者
謝如意
總編輯
黃淑惠

翻譯
何久恩、陳美君
文稿協助
賴燕貞、郭心怡、王志偉
馬優雅、絲黛安、梁偉業、陳素真

攝影
大野現
美術編輯
張菲
封面設計
王瑾
設計協助
黃雯雯

電腦排版
三原色設計工作室
分色製版
豐泰分色製版公司
印刷
福茂彩色印刷公司

味全出版社有限公司
台北市仁愛路四段 28 號 2 樓
電話：2702-1148 · 2702-1149
傳真：2704-2729

郵政劃撥 00182038 號
味全出版社帳戶

版權所有：局版台業字第 0179 號
2002 年 9 月初版　1-0-8
定價：新台幣參佰元整

Author
Christina Sjahir Hwang
Editor
Su-Huei Huang

Translation
John Holt, Meghan Chen
Editorial Staff
Yen-Jen Lai, Margaret Kuo, Chi Wai Wong , Gloria Martinez,
Diane Soliz-Martese, Jarrod Leung, Su-Jen Chen

Photography
Aki Ohno
Art Direction
Faye Chang
Cover Design
Chin Ong
Art and Production Assistant
Vivian Huang

Printed in Taiwan

Wei-Chuan Publishing
1455 Monterey Pass Rd., #110
Monterey Park, CA 91754, U.S.A.
Tel: 323 · 261 · 3880 · 323 · 261 · 3878
Fax: 323 · 261 · 3299
www.weichuancookbook.com

Notice: Information contained in this book is accurate and
complete to the best of our knowledge. All recommendations are
made with no guarantees on the part of the author or Wei-Chuan
Publishing. The author and publisher disclaim all liability in
connection with the use or misuse of this information.

FIRST PRINTING: SEPTEMBER 2002
ISBN: 0-941676-82-X
(Chinese/English)

7 16598 00082 6

目錄 CONTENTS

生於印尼蘇門答島

的我，是印尼華裔第三代。自小喜好烹調藝術，早年常隨先母在廚房打轉，稍長後更向當地名師學習廚藝。1968年負笈台灣，雖攻讀商科，但對烹飪之興趣卻有增無減。在台求學期間~60年代末的台灣，因飲食未趨國際化，無處可嚐家鄉的南國風味菜餚，於是每逢暑假返家之餘，必鑽研傳統南洋菜餚之調理，以便返校後能解嘴饞。當年台灣、日本、韓國等地的同學對星、馬、印等地的菜餚並不熟悉，甚至未曾嚐過。因此每當宿舍裡飄出獨特的南洋菜香，同學莫不聞香而至，嚐過之後方知南國菜餚也是別具一番風味。1985年移居美國後，更發現星、馬、印，尤其是印尼對西方人士而言，似乎是蒙上了一層神秘的面紗，人們對其歷史、風俗習慣、飲食及文化等背景毫無概念。所謂：「欲瞭解一國的文化，必先了解其飲食」。因此，本人一直希望能將大半生鑽研之南國佳餚做一系統介紹，讓世人對南洋島國之飲食有深層的瞭解。由於外子及兩個女兒不斷的鼓勵，在付出時間及努力耕耘後，南洋菜這本食譜終於問世。希望本食譜能對促進東西飲食文化交流有所貢獻。

在此特別感謝黃淑惠女士對我的支持及味全出版社編輯組的鼎力相助。也謝謝印尼駐洛山磯總領事館與新加坡旅遊局在攝影背景方面所提供的傳統文物。並感謝好友杜麗華、小姑黃鸝、黃凰、胞妹謝如華在蒐集資料中給予的協助，更要感謝外子黃大、女兒黃筱甯及黃筱淨在這一年來著作過程中給予的精神支持與關懷，使這本食譜得以順利完成。為了能讓讀者就地取材，本書特別精選了68道材料採購方便、步驟簡化、美味又具有代表性之佳餚，希望能得到讀者的喜愛。最後願與本人任教的成人學校烹飪班同學分享這本食譜。

謹以本書獻給今年剛滿80歲的家父謝章武，因您早年的啟發、栽培及鼓勵，才有這本食譜的面世，謝謝您！

A third generation Chinese born in Sumatra, Indonesia, I grew up surrounded by the fabulously exotic aromas and tastes of the Southeast Asian dishes prepared by my mother. From her, I developed a lifelong passion for cooking and the exploration of the many diverse and subtle flavors of the cuisine of Singapore, Malaysia and Indonesia.

While studying business in Taiwan in 1968, I continued my culinary development by preparing the meals of my homeland. I soon discovered that the aromas emanating from my kitchen were drawing my Taiwanese, Korean, and Japanese friends to my door for a new culinary experience. Their demonstrated delight in the dishes inspired me to explore even deeper the secrets of Southeast Asian cooking, leading me to study with well known chefs during my spare time.

After immigrating to the United States in 1985, I soon learned that the cuisines of Singapore, Malaysia and Indonesia were practically unknown. Accordingly, I have prepared the recipes in this cookbook to introduce the Western palate to the succulent, aromatic and exotic tastes of Southeast Asia. There are sixty-eight specially selected recipes that represent the breadth and variety of cuisine of my homeland. The recipes are easy to follow and call for ingredients readily available or easily substituted.

Thanks to my husband Howard Hwang and our daughters Natalie and Cindy, for their moral support and encouragement. I am especially grateful to Ms. Su-Huei Huang and the staff at Wei-Chuan Publishing for their tireless support and editorial guidance. I also thank the Indonesian Consulate and the Singaporean Tourist Bureau for availing to us cultural artifacts that appear in the photographs. Without the research assistance of my friends and family, this cookbook would not have been possible; my heartfelt gratitude to them – Hilda Toh, Lee Hwang, Katherine Hwang, and Catherine Sjahir. I share the joy of this work with my students at the adult cooking school where I teach.

I dedicate this cookbook to my father, Budisarso Sjahir, who celebrated his 80th birthday this year. I thank you, father, for piquing my curiosity, availing education to me, and encouraging me to persist. Without you, this book would not have become a reality. It is my hope the reader will fully enjoy this cookbook.

星加坡

位居馬來半島最南端的星加坡為東南亞最小的國家,人口僅三百萬左右,但卻是亞洲四小龍之一。經濟繁榮,高樓大廈林立,巨型百貨公司販售著世界各地的舶來品。由於政府完善的規劃,市容堪稱東南亞之最,著名小吃更是讓人津津樂道,因此,被譽為旅遊天堂。

星加坡是國際飲食的大熔爐,它在飲食文化方面呈現的多元特性,主要是受到當地濃厚的殖民與移民色彩,而擁有多元種族及文化,包括中國、馬來西亞、印尼及印度等等的影響;其人口結構中,華裔約佔75%,馬來裔佔15%,印度裔佔6%,其他族裔佔4%。因此中國

娘惹菜是星加坡最具代表性的料理。其源自於早年中國男人與馬來族女人通婚後,馬來太太採用中式材料配上馬來調味、香料、香草葉,並以辛辣醬料加上椰奶烹調而成。娘惹菜味道獨特,有濃厚的南洋風味,辣度適中,不僅迎合了中國男人的胃口,也不失其原有的馬來風味,是值得一嚐的菜餚。本書中也特別介紹了變通的娘惹菜,以便讀者對當地特殊的飲食有更深的認識。

星加坡多元的飲食文化充份反映在一般家庭的用餐方式上,譬如早餐可以是牛奶麥片或印度麵包,中餐是中式便餐,晚餐則為傳統的馬來菜餚,再加上一道中式

菜、馬來/印尼菜、印度菜及中馬合一的娘惹菜是當地最為盛行的。

中國菜在星加坡佔有一席之地,在此可以嚐盡中國各地的美食佳餚;而市面上小吃攤隨處可見的各種中國南方傳統風味小吃,是由早年中國東南沿海福建、廣東等南移的中國人帶到星加坡的。其烹調方式與一般中國菜無異,仍以炒、蒸、滷、燉等方式加以變化,調味方面,惟受潮州菜式影響,特別喜用豆醬。

馬來/印尼與印度菜,在當地亦非常流行。從英國殖民時代印度士兵的後裔到鄰國爪哇、蘇門答臘、馬都拉等島湧進來的馬來族裔,都將他們傳統的飲食文化帶進來。印、馬菜及印度菜大量使用辣椒及香料,配上濃郁的椰奶烹調而成,這種香辣的獨特口味,令人百吃不厭,回味無窮。

熱湯,廚房裡交融著烤沙嗲味,香蒜味及咖哩味,可謂五味雜陳。用餐時以米飯為主,配上幾道菜餚,及一般家庭必備的三峇辣椒沾醬,按各自喜好選用。除米飯及湯類保持溫熱外,其他菜餚保持室溫即可。故馬來/印尼、印度及娘惹菜,除青菜外,多數可事先燒好,需要時隨時取食。又、匙、碗、盤為常用餐具,宴客時需備妥公匙,但有以傳統馬來方式用手抓食者也不足為奇。

星加坡以其廉能有效的政府、整潔的環境、良好的治安與現代化的花園市容聞名於世,琳琅滿目的小吃更是令人食指大動,尤其是*海南雞飯、星式喇沙、肉骨茶、蝦麵、烤魚餅、南洋薄餅、辣醬螃蟹、印度炒麵、木薯椰奶糕、椰茸糯米球*等等,您要是去了星加坡,可千萬不能錯過。

Singapore 在中譯上,因各地用字與語言習慣的不同,有譯成 "新加坡"、"星加坡" 或 "星洲"。為了使本食譜內文字編排能有一致性,故選用 "星加坡" 為本書統一之中譯名稱。

SINGAPORE

Located on the southern tip of the Malaysian peninsula, Singapore is the smallest nation in Southeast Asia. Although small, Singapore is recognized as one of the economic forces in Asia. Towering skyscrapers and gigantic shopping malls with imports from markets of the world serve as a testament to Singapore's bustling economy. This tropical island-state boasts order, safety, and delectable "street food." It is a renowned haven for tourists.

Singapore is an international culinary melting pot, blending many cultural influences from indigenous people as well as immigrants from China, Malaysia, Indonesia, and India. The most popular fares reflect this cultural diversity.

Chinese cuisine enjoys center stage in Singapore. One may savor exquisite dishes from every famous region in China and a variety of delicious "street food" boasting traditional flavors from southeast China provinces of *Guangdong* and *Fujian*. Immigrants from these provinces brought with them such cooking techniques as stir-frying, steaming, braising, and slow stewing. The *Chao-Zhou* influence has made preserved soybeans the preferred flavoring agent.

Malaysian/Indonesian and Indian dishes are prominent in Singapore. These cultural manifestations are derived from Malaysian descendants from Java, Sumatra, and Madura islands and the descendants of Indian soldiers from the British colonial era. Characteristics of this cuisine are large quantities of chilies and spices, laced with rich coconut milk.

Nyonya cuisine, the most symbolic of all Singaporean cooking, is a unique confluence of Chinese and Malaysian flavors. As Chinese men inter-married with local Malaysian women, the women prepared dishes that suited their husbands' taste buds and yet were able to retain the traditional Malaysian native flavors. These women dressed Chinese ingredients with Malaysian spices, fragrant herbs, spicy pastes and sauces, and rich coconut milk. The results are a unique blend of exciting flavors and tempered spices as featured in the variations of Nyonya cuisine.

The family kitchen reflects the variety of Singaporean cuisine. Breakfast consists of milk, oatmeal, or Indian bread; Lunch is a Chinese combination quick meal; Dinner consists of traditional Malaysian dishes and a Chinese soup to complement the meal. A typical meal includes steamed rice, served with a few dishes, and the requisite *Sambal chili sauces*. While the steamed rice and hot soup are served warm, other dishes may be served at room temperature. Malaysian/ Indonesian, Indian, and Nyonya dishes, except for vegetables, may be prepared ahead of time. Forks, spoons, bowls, and dishes are commonly used to set the table, although some Malaysian dishes are enjoyed by using the fingers of the hand.

Singapore is famous for its food stands that offer a myriad of dishes to excite the curious palate. Especially memorable are *Hainan Chicken Rice, Noodles in Spicy Coconut Milk Soup, Sparerib Soup, Prawn Noodle Soup, Fish Cakes in Banana Leaves, Hokkienese Spring Rolls, Spicy Crab, Indian Fried Noodles, Steamed Cassava Cake, and Sweet Coconut Rice Balls* and more. A visit to Singapore would be regrettably incomplete if one bypassed tasting these dishes!

Courtesy of the Singaporean Tourist Bureau

印尼 及 馬來西亞

千島之國印尼(印度尼西亞)，位居於東南亞與澳洲之間，是由 13,667 個島嶼所組成，為世界上最大而延伸最長的群島國家。人口約 1 億九仟萬，大多聚集在爪哇、蘇門答臘、加里曼丹等大島上，坐稱世界第四大人口國。印尼擁有世界百分之六十的熱帶雨林，因雨量充沛，也造就了遍地綠野、一望無際的稻田與茂密的橡膠園，天然純樸的原始風貌為其特色。

位於印尼西北邊、同樣以原始自然景觀著稱的馬來西亞，是由馬來半島(西馬)、沙巴和砂勞越(東馬)組成。馬來半島位居印尼蘇門答臘島東北方，僅一馬六甲海峽之隔，而東馬則位於北加里曼丹島(中及南加里曼丹屬印尼)。兩國鄰近的地理位置，加上幾近相同的氣候、歷史、文化背景、風俗習慣及族裔，可稱為兄弟國。

印尼諸島和馬來西亞地處樞紐，加上盛產香料和擁有豐富的天然資源，自古以來即為兵家必爭之地，也因此造就了印、馬兩國多元種族的文化特色～以印尼和馬來人為主，次為中國人，印度及其他族裔如英國、葡萄牙、荷蘭及阿拉伯人；且兩國皆為殖民色彩濃厚的國家～馬來西亞曾淪為英國殖民地，至 1957 年方獨立；印尼曾被荷蘭統治長達三百年，二戰期間又被日本佔領長達三年，於 1945 年獨立。因此，當地的飲食文化深受各地移民、殖民者的影響而呈現多元性，而兩國的飲食文化更是有密切的關連。

由於受到多元文化的洗禮，異國的烹煮文化也融入了當地，在馬來西亞，以馬來菜、中國菜、印度菜為主，而在華人聚集的地區如檳城和吉隆坡，中馬合一的娘惹菜(見第六頁星加坡)也頗為盛行。

印尼則除了異國飲食文化外，當地島嶼上都各有其傳統、獨特的菜餚。蘇門答臘菜，因與中東及印度香料商有直接接觸，在烹調上較廣泛的使用各種香料來搭配大量的辣椒，尤其是蘇門答臘西部的巴東菜，以大辣、味濃著稱，是全印尼膾炙人口的佳餚，在星、馬一帶也頗盛行。爪哇菜帶有特殊少數民族的風情，善用蝦醬提

Courtesy of the Indonesian Consulate, Los Angeles

味，配上各式各樣的香草葉，口味偏甜，辣度溫和，常見以香蕉葉包裹各種材料烹調，上桌打開時帶有蕉葉的清香，而以香蘭葉及椰奶烹製的甜點，更帶有濃郁的香味。這是印尼最具代表性的兩種傳統菜餚。

由於印尼及馬來西亞兩國皆因長年處在炎熱潮濕的環境，人們偏好辛辣食物以刺激胃口，因此辣椒對當地人堪稱"十全大補劑"。烹煮過程中，大量使用辣椒，配上當地盛產的辛香料及椰奶，煮成濃郁而帶有辣味與椰奶香的菜餚，而辣椒的先用、後用、多辣或少辣能創造出變化無窮的口味。

米飯為印、馬兩國的主食，早餐有炒飯、椰奶飯、飯糰配上幾道小菜，加上一杯甜茶或咖啡加煉奶；午晚餐則以米飯為主，配上開胃的泡菜與四至五道的各式菜餚，如椰汁蔬菜湯、牛或雞肉咖哩、辣椒魚、酸辣蝦等等；佐以不同的辣醬如三峇辣醬等，再配上炸蝦片或撒些香味配料如油蔥酥等在菜餚上。出菜時同時上桌，無所謂冷熱之分。由於多數印、馬菜有「越煮越香」的特性，一般家庭主婦僅在上午調理一日份之菜餚，宴客時可在前幾天先做好大部份，屆時取出熱過即可。一般印、馬原住民仍以傳統方式用手抓飯吃，因此桌上常備有一碗清水作為飯前清洗右手之用；而現代化家庭則以叉、匙、盤子為常用的餐具，並備有「公匙」。

在印、馬的街頭巷尾有不計其數的小攤子、小吃店及沿街叫賣的小販，販售著各式各樣道地風味的小吃，從烤沙爹、烤大蝦，爪哇沙拉、檳城喇沙、牛尾湯、咖哩牛肉、香辣炒麵及各種糕點等等，真是琳琅滿目令人垂涎。夜市更是市民夜間流連的好去處，置身於熙來攘往的小巷中，大吃大嚼，夾雜著四面八方飄來的烤肉串香味，還真別有一番情趣。坐在椰樹下，來顆嫩椰，吸口清涼的椰汁，保証暑氣全消，如此南國情調，令人陶醉其中！閒暇之餘，何不換個口味嚐嚐香辣、濃郁的印、馬佳餚呢？

Located between Southeast Asia and Australia, Indonesia is comprised of 13,667 islands, making it the largest, most expansive nation of islands in the world. Ranked as the fourth largest population of the world, the majority of Indonesia's population inhabits the larger islands of *Java, Sumatra, and Kalimantan (Borneo)*. Indonesia possesses sixty percent of the world's tropical rain forests.

Malaysia is northwest of Indonesia and is comprised of the *Malay Peninsula (West Malaysia)* and *Sabah* and *Sarawak (East Malaysia)*. *West Malaysia* is located on the northeast side of Indonesia's Island of *Sumatra*, separated by the *Malaka Strait*. East Malaysia is actually on north *Kalimantan* (middle and south *Kalimantan* belong to Indonesia). Because of the geographic proximity and similarities in climate, culture, history, customs, and ethnic groups, Indonesia and Malaysia are like sister nations.

The Indonesian islands and Malaysia are situated along an often traveled route, their great variety of spices and rich natural resources have made them subject to conquest. These conquests produced people of various ethnicities and races, each leaving its cultural imprint on Indonesia and Malaysia. The cultural diversity of both nations consists mainly of indigenous Indonesian and Malaysian peoples, followed by Chinese, Indian, British, Portuguese, Dutch, and Arab. Therefore, both nations' culture and cuisine are intimately related as both have been profoundly influenced by the continual influx of various peoples.

In Malaysia, the main cuisine is Malaysian, Chinese, and Indian. In ethnic Chinese enclaves such as *Penang* and *Kuala Lumpur,* the merging of Malaysian and Chinese cuisine - Nyonya cuisine, (see page 6 "Singapore") - is also very popular .

Indonesian cuisine is characterized by foreign influences, while traditional fares unique to each island, also lay claim to national fame. The generous use of chilies combined with Middle Eastern and Indian spices characterizes the cuisine of Sumatra. Padang cuisine, famous for rich, savory tasting spices and hot chilies, is widely enjoyed in all of Indonesia, Singapore and Malaysia. The cuisine of Java boasts of its unique use of shrimp paste, accompanied by various fragrant spices and herbs, which yield slightly sweet, temperate chili tastes.

Due to their humid and hot tropical climate, Indonesians and Malaysians use great quantities of chilies and spices to stimulate their appetites. Chilies are considered highly beneficial for maintaining good health. The chilies may be used at any point in the cooking process, and the amount may be adjusted to produce a great variety of flavors.

Rice is the main staple in both Indonesia and Malaysia. Breakfast consists of fried rice, coconut rice, and/or rice balls accompanied by several small dishes, and a cup of sweet tea or coffee with sweet condensed milk. Lunch and dinner begin with pickled salad to awaken a hearty appetite. This is followed by steamed rice accompanied by four to five dishes, such as coconut vegetable soup, curry beef or chicken, chili fish, and hot-and-sour shrimp. Enriching the taste of these dishes are various chili pastes such as *Sambal chili sauce*, fried shrimp chips, or crispy fried green onions to garnish the dishes.

Because numerous Indonesian and Malaysian dishes taste even better the longer they are cooked, most housewives prepare an entire day's meals in the morning, reheating the dishes as they are needed throughout the day. When hosting a meal, most of the dishes may be prepared a few days in advance and reheated when the guests arrive. Most Indonesian and Malaysian natives use fingers to eat. Therefore, a bowl of clean water is placed on the dining table to cleanse hands before eating. The more modern households see the use of forks, spoons, and plates, as well as serving spoons, on the dining table.

Another way to enjoy Indonesian and Malaysian cuisine is less formal – food stands. A multitude of food stands, little eateries, and mobile food carts can be found on the streets and alleys of Indonesia and Malaysia. It is indeed a delightful sight and a feast for salivating palates. The tropical nights bring out large crowds of street food addicts, roaming while sampling the many delicacies, amidst compelling fragrances that lure the diners to move on to the next dishes. A truly satisfying culinary experience enjoyed by the more adventurous food lovers and connoisseurs.

量器介紹
MEASURING TOOLS

1 杯（1 飯碗）=16 大匙
1 c. (1 cup) = 236 c.c.

量調味料時，請用標準量器。所有食譜內的材料，除有特別指示外，均為洗過、削皮後或處理過的淨重。

Use proper measuring tools to ensure accuracy of amounts of ingredients used. Unless specified, all ingredients listed in recipes are washed, peeled, or otherwise prepared to yield net weights.

1 大匙（1 湯匙）
1 T. (1 Tablespoon) = 15 c.c.

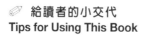
✎ **給讀者的小交代**
Tips for Using This Book

炸的時間長短通常和所用的鍋子材質、火力大小及油量多寡等有關。本食譜內炸的時間及火候，是依據美國一般家庭所使用的瓦斯爐試作的，讀者可依此做參考，自行加減炸的時間，以得最好的效果。

1 小匙（1 茶匙）
1 t. (1 teaspoon) = 5 c.c.

The time for deep-frying is determined by the type of pots, degree of heat, and quantity of oil used. The specifications in this cookbook for time of frying and degree of heat are based on gas stoves. Readers may use this cookbook as a reference and adjust frying time as preferred.

特殊材料 及 調味料
SPECIAL INGREDIENTS AND SEASONINGS

香蕉葉
可當盤子裝盛食物，或用以包肉類或點心，經蒸或烤出來後帶有獨特的蕉葉味，可增加食物的美味。

椰奶
椰果肉或椰茸加水攪爛過濾擠出即為椰奶，靜置後浮在上面的即為濃椰奶。若用罐裝，需先搖勻再開罐。濃椰奶是未經搖勻，凝在上面的白色固體。

椰茸
椰果肉刨成絲，有冷凍椰茸出售。可用來炒或做成各式各樣的點心。

香蕉葉
banana leaves

椰奶
coconut milk

椰茸
shredded coconut

Banana leaves
May be used as a plate to serve food or to wrap meat dishes or desserts. When baked or steamed, the banana leaf flavor enhances the taste of the dishes.

Coconut milk
Coconut flesh or coconut shreds blended thoroughly with water, then strained to yield coconut milk. Set aside and the top layer of the milk curdles and becomes thick coconut milk. If using canned coconut milk, shake well prior to opening. The thick coconut milk is the curdled, unshaken portion of the contents.

Shredded coconut
Also available in the frozen food section of Asian markets. May be used to make small dishes or various desserts.

蝦米
曬乾的小蝦仁，用來炒菜、煮湯，增加菜餚的鮮味。

蝦米
dried shrimp

椰子糖
從棕櫚樹花蕾提煉出來的，有濃濃的焦糖味。使用時用刀壓碎或加少許水稀釋。

豆醬
以黃豆為主要材料，味鹹，以瓶裝出售，是潮州菜常用的材料之一。星加坡菜也常用豆醬來調味，若無可用日本味噌取代。

椰子糖
palm sugar

蝦醬
小蝦與鹽混合製成，味鹹有刺鼻味，可增加食物的鮮味。

甜醬油
味甜的濃醬油，除當調味品外，也可當沾醬。

豆醬
preserved soybeans

酸子
一種味酸的天然果實。市面上買來的酸子 1 杯加熱水 5 杯泡軟，過濾擠出濃汁即為酸子汁，可裝在容器內置冰箱保存數週。酸子汁用來調酸味及加深菜餚顏色並使成濃稠狀。若無法購得酸子，可用其他帶有酸味的果汁，如漬酸梅或青檸檬汁替代。

蝦醬
shrimp paste

Dried shrimp
Sun dried shrimp, used to flavor dishes and soups.

Palm sugar
Made from palm flowers; tastes and smells like caramelized sugar. Use a knife to flatten or mix with water to loosen before using.

Preserved soybeans
Made of soybeans with a salty taste and sold in jars; commonly used in Chao-Zhou dishes as well as Singaporean dishes. If preserved soybeans are not available, Japanese miso can be substituted.

甜醬油
sweet soy sauce

Shrimp paste
A mixture of mashed small shrimp and salt, yielding a savory flavor to enhance any dish. It is sold in a jar.

Sweet soy sauce
Sweet and thickened soy sauce to flavor dishes and used as a dipping sauce.

Tamarind
A tart fruit. Available in markets, add 5 cups of hot water to 1 cup tamarind; strain. May be refrigerated for several weeks. Tamarind juice is used to darken the hue of certain dishes, give acidity, and to thicken sauces. If tamarind is not available, other acidic fruit juices may be substituted as well as preserved palm juice or lime juice.

酸子
tamarind

辛香料 · 香草葉 · 香料
FRAGRANT SPICES AND HERBS

九層塔
basil

法國香葉
bay leaves

臘仁
candlenuts

小豆蔻
cardamom

辣椒
chili peppers

九層塔
有紫色及綠色幹兩種九層塔，南洋菜中所使用的是味道較淡的綠色幹。

法國香葉
月桂樹的乾葉，一般用在有湯汁的菜餚內，或放入油內炒，以增香味。

臘仁
米色堅硬的果仁，含有豐富的油脂，可增加菜餚中的油質並使湯汁濃稠。

小豆蔻
米色，有怡人香味的小果實，用在米飯及咖哩菜餚以增加香味。

辣椒
辣椒有紅、綠兩色，可使菜餚有辣味，也可當裝飾。小辣椒比大辣椒辣，可按自己的喜好來選擇辣椒的種類。

肉桂
黃褐色的乾燥樹皮，味道刺激，可用整支肉桂或將其磨成粉使用。

丁香
熱帶植物的乾花苞，有刺鼻的香味。可整粒或磨成粉使用。

芫荽子粉
芫荽的種子磨成粉，是燒烤類最佳的調味料，娘惹菜中也常用它為香料。

小茴香子
有刺鼻濃郁的香味，是咖哩香料中的主要成份。

Basil
Available in purple-stem and green-stem varieties; Southeast Asian cuisine use the green variety.

Bay leaves
Dried, aromatic leaf of the laurel-like shrub, used in dishes with sauces or for stir-frying to enhance flavor.

Candlenuts
Beige, hard fruit with a rich oil content; may be used to enrich dishes and to thicken sauces.

Cardamom
Small, beige, sweet scented fruit; used in rice and curry dishes to enhance aroma.

Chili peppers
Green or red chili peppers make any dish hot; also used to garnish. Smaller chili peppers are hotter than larger ones; select according to personal taste.

Cinnamon
Golden brown, dried skin of spice tree; has a strong aroma. Often used in cut pieces or powder form.

Cloves
Tropical flower pods; have a sweet-smelling aroma; used whole or ground.

Coriander powder
Made from coriander pods, best used for broiled and grilled dishes. Also commonly used in Nyonya cuisine.

Cumin
Has a distinctive flavor, which is the major ingredient in curry spice.

肉桂
cinnamon sticks

丁香
cloves

芫荽子粉
coriander powder

小茴香子
cumin

南薑 / Galangal

與薑同類,味辛香,炒過後濃濃的香味能去除肉類的腥味。可買冷凍的代替新鮮南薑較為經濟,使用時以刀背略拍或攪碎成泥。

A ginger variety with a special fragrance. When stir-fried, enlivens meat dishes. Frozen galangal is cheaper than fresh. Lightly crush or mash before use.

南薑
galangal

檸檬葉 / Kaffir leaves

是皺皮檸檬的葉子。檸檬葉所散發出來的香味加在咖哩、辛辣菜餚中即能達到南洋菜獨特風味的效果。

Leaves of the wrinkled lemon tree; a special fragrance added to curry and spicy hot dishes to give Southeast Asian cuisine its unique identity.

檸檬葉
kaffir leaves

辣草葉 / Knotgrass

俗稱越南芫荽,具有特別濃郁的辛香味,最適用於調理海鮮類,新鮮葉子可用來拌飯或撒入湯麵內。

Commonly known as Vietnamese coriander, its sharpness suits seafood dishes. Fresh leaves may be mixed with rice or used to garnish noodle soups.

辣草葉
knotgrass

香茅 / Lemon grass

具有獨特的香味。使用時只取其根部 6-8 寸長,撕去外圍的硬葉,僅其嫩根部,用刀拍扁以便烹煮時能將香味徹底發揮出來。

Produces a unique flavor; use only the 6-8 inches above its root. Tear off the tough outer layer; crush the soft inner core with the side of a knife to release its full flavor.

香茅
lemon grass

豆蔻 / Nutmeg

深棕色堅硬的果實,拍碎或磨成粉使用,其獨特的香味,常用於點心的香料或做菜的調味料。

Deep brown fruit in a hard shell. Crush or grind to use, suitable for desserts or seasoning.

豆蔻
nutmeg

香蘭葉 / Pandan leaves

其香味用於增添餐點的香濃,市面上可買到冷凍的。香蘭葉常用在米飯或點心內,而香蘭精則用來著色。

Used to intensify the flavor of many dishes, such as rice or desserts. Frozen leaves are available in markets. Pandan extract is used for coloring.

紅蔥頭 / Shallots

體形較洋蔥小,攪碎成泥後可做為烹飪常用的材料,經酥炸後可做為香味配料。

Smaller than brown onions; grind to a paste to season any dish. Deep-fried shallots (crispy shallots) may be used to garnish dishes.

黃薑粉 / Turmeric powder

黃薑磨成粉即為黃薑粉,黃薑粉為深黃色,多用來著色,因味濃不宜多用。

Finely ground turmeric has a deep yellow hue. It is used primarily for adding color; use sparingly due to its strong flavor.

黃薑粉
turmeric powder

紅蔥頭
shallots

香蘭葉
pandan leaves

高湯介紹
STOCK

使用雞、豬、牛或海鮮的肉或骨頭剁塊，放入清水內煮數小時出來的湯，稱為高湯。因高湯含有美味的精華，除用來煮湯外，更可用來烹調各種菜餚，使煮出來的菜餚增加美味，甚至煮飯時，均可使用高湯來取代清水。以雞、豬、或牛骨熬煮成的高湯，通常用來烹調肉類為主的菜餚，以海鮮煮成的高湯，通常用來烹調以海鮮類為主的菜餚。

為了使熬出來的高湯純淨不混濁，熬高湯時需隨時將浮上的雜質撈出。做好的高湯若不喜油脂，待冷後放入冰箱過夜，再把凝固的浮油去掉，就可有完全無油、澄清的高湯。做高湯時不妨多做，再分為五杯一包冰凍備用。

煮好的高湯，可隨喜好加入雞精、牛肉精或魚精，增加高湯的美味。若臨時需要而沒有高湯時，亦可以雞精、牛肉精或用魚精加水來代替各種高湯。

The prepared stock flavor may be enhanced with chicken, beef, or fish bouillon. If stock is not on hand, bouillon mixed with water may be used.

Made from chicken, pork, beef, seafood, or bones slowly cooked in water. Because stock is flavorful, it is commonly used for soups and to enrich the flavor of any dish. Stock may be substituted for water when cooking rice. Stock made from chicken, pork, or beef tend to be used with meat dishes, seafood stock with seafood dishes.

To ensure a clear stock, skim foam from stock. If fat-free stock is preferred, chill stock overnight in the refrigerator and skim fat from the stock. A large quantity may be prepared and frozen in five-cup portions for future use.

肉高湯
全雞、雞、豬或牛骨
2 斤 4 兩(1350 公克)

將材料剁塊，隨意加蔥薑與 20 杯水燒開，撈出浮在湯面的泡沫，改小火蓋鍋煮 2 1/2 小時後，將骨頭及雜質撈出，約可得 10 杯。

海鮮高湯
魚頭、魚尾、魚骨頭、蝦頭、蝦殼　共 1 斤 8 兩(900 公克)

將材料隨意加蔥、薑與 15 杯水燒開，撈出浮在湯面上的泡沫，改小火蓋鍋煮 2 小時後，將骨頭及雜質撈出過濾，約可得 10 杯。

MEAT STOCK
3 lbs. (1350g) whole chicken or bones of chicken, pork, or beef

Cut ingredients into chunks. Add green onions and ginger with 20 cups of water; bring to boil. Skim foam from stock; reduce heat to low. Cover and simmer for 2 1/2 hours. Remove meat and bones; strain stock to yield about 10 cups.

SEAFOOD STOCK
Total 2 lbs. (900g) fish bones (head, tail), shrimp heads and shells

Add green onions and ginger with 15 cups of water; bring to boil. Skim foam from stock; reduce heat to low. Cover and simmer two hours. Remove all ingredients; strain stock to yield about 10 cups.

香味配料
AROMATIC CONDIMENTS

香味配料為南洋菜的獨特風味之一，常用來撒在做好的菜餚上面或加入湯內以增加香味。香味配料香酥的口感，不但使菜餚更加美味可口，又可以做為盤飾。書內常使用的香味配料為下列三種：

Aromatic condiments are one of the hallmarks of Southeast Asian cuisine and are commonly used as toppings to enhance dishes. The crispy, fried flavor not only enhances the taste of dishes, but also serves as a garnish. The most commonly used are these three types:

油蔥酥、蒜頭酥和
炸過的花生可在市面上
買到現成的，但風味
不及自製的好，所以使用前
可以略為炒香以增加香味。

Crispy garlic, crispy shallots, and ground peanuts are available in Asian markets; however, homemade versions are superior. To improve taste, first lightly stir-fry, then serve.

油蔥酥
紅蔥頭切成薄片，放入油內以中火炸至香酥，表面呈淡褐色撈出濾乾油。

蒜頭酥
紅蔥頭切成薄片，放入油內以中火炸至香酥，表面呈淡褐色撈出濾乾油。

碎花生
將炸好的花生仁壓碎。

CRISPY SHALLOTS
Thinly sliced shallots, deep-fried in medium heat until crispy and golden brown; Drain.

CRISPY GARLIC
Thinly sliced garlic, deep-fried in medium heat until crispy and golden brown; Drain.

GROUND PEANUTS
Deep-fried then coarsely ground.

泡菜
PICKLED SALADS

將醃漬材料混合放入冰箱數小時，冰涼後即可享用，可當飯前開胃小菜或配飯小菜。

Marinated and chilled ahead of time, pickled salads may be served as appetizers or accompaniments to any meal.

南洋泡菜

黃瓜（去籽切條）	1 杯
紅蘿蔔（切條）	3/4 杯
紅蔥頭（切塊）	6 個
小辣椒	12 支
水	1 1/2 大匙
醋	3 大匙
糖	2 大匙
鹽	1 1/4 小匙

FRESH VEGETABLE PICKLES
(Acar Segar)

1 c.	cucumber (seeded, cut in strips)
3/4 c.	carrot (cut in strips)
6	shallots (diced)
12	bird's eye chili peppers
1 1/2 T.	water
3 T.	vinegar
2 T.	sugar
1 1/4 t.	salt

酸辣黃瓜鳳梨

黃瓜（去籽切丁）	1 杯
鳳梨丁	1 杯
紅蔥頭（切薄片）	2 個
辣椒（切片）	2 支
鹽	1 1/4 小匙
糖	2 大匙
青檸檬汁	3 大匙

CUCUMBER & PINEAPPLE PICKLES
(Acar Nanas Ketimum)

1 c.	cucumber (seeded, diced)
1 c.	pineapple (diced)
2	shallots (sliced)
2	chili peppers (sliced)
1 1/4 t.	salt
2 T.	sugar
3 T.	lime juice

三峇辣醬
SAMBAL CHILI SAUCES

辣椒的形狀大小及其辣味差別很大，喜辣者可使用細小辣椒及粗大辣椒各半混合使用，不喜太辣者則僅用大辣椒即可。

The size, shape, and degree of spiciness varies greatly among chili peppers. Those who enjoy very spicy tastes may use a mixture of small and large chili peppers. Those who prefer medium hotness may use only the large peppers.

三峇辣醬是南洋菜最具特色的醬料，通常用來直接淋、拌或沾食，其香濃獨特的辣味讓人食指大動、胃口大開。印尼、馬來人所稱的"三峇"指的就是各種不同口味的辣醬，有的味道香濃，帶有蝦醬味；有的辣中帶酸，別具風味。三峇辣醬的做法很簡單，只要將辣椒、辛香料及調味一起搗碎拌勻即成，可一次多做裝入密封罐中冷藏保存

Sambal chili sauces characterize Southeast Asian cuisine. Dripped over dishes, mixed with other ingredients, or for dipping, the sauces' spicy character excites appetites and enhances the enjoyment of any dish. Commonly used in Indonesia and Malaysia, the term "Sambal" refers to various chili pastes. Some are very spicy, others have shrimp paste flavoring, still others are hot-and-sour. Sambal chili sauces are easy to prepare: just mash and blend chili peppers and spices. A large quantity may be prepared ahead of time and refrigerated in airtight jars for future use.

蝦醬味辣醬

SHRIMP PASTE SAMBAL
Sambal Terasi/Belacan

① 辣椒、蕃茄 共 4 兩 (150 公克)	
② 蝦醬、椰子糖 各 1 大匙 鹽 1/8 小匙 (口味淡者可省略)	
青檸檬汁 1 大匙	

① 1/3 lb. (150g) total: chili peppers, tomatoes	
② 1 T. ea.: shrimp paste, palm sugar 1/8 t. salt (optional)	
1 T. lime juice	

將 ① 料以開水燙熟，加 ② 料用杵搗碎或用機器攪碎，拌入青檸檬汁即成。此乃南洋菜中常用的沾醬，不論生菜、炸魚、炸雞、炸豆腐及炒飯都可沾食。

Blanch ① in boiling water; remove to a mortar and pestle or blender, add ② then grind. Mix with lime juice. This is the most commonly used sauce in households, and accompanies uncooked vegetables, fried fish, fried chicken, fried tofu, and fried rice.

酸醋辣醬   VINEGAR SAMBAL *Sambal Cuka*

1	辣椒	4 兩 (150 公克)
	蒜頭	6 瓣
2	鹽	1/4 小匙
	醋	1 大匙

1	1/3 lb. (150g)	chili peppers
	6	garlic cloves
2	1/4 t.	salt
	1 T.	vinegar

將 1 料搗碎或攪碎再拌入 2 料即成。炒麵及湯麵均可配此辣醬。

Grind 1 with a mortar and pestle or blender; add 2 and mix well. This sauce may be used with fried noodles or noodle soups.

甜辣醬   SWEET SAMBAL *Sambal Kecap Manis*

小辣椒 (切碎)	3 支
甜醬油	3 大匙
青檸檬汁	1 大匙

3	bird's eye chili peppers
3 T.	sweet soy sauce
1 T.	lime juice

將所有材料混合拌勻即成。可配各種牛肉湯或羊肉湯裡的肉塊。

Mix all ingredients well. This sauce may be used as a dipping sauce for beef or lamb chunks from soups.

花生辣醬   PEANUT SAMBAL *Sambal Kacang*

1	辣椒	4 支
	蒜頭	6 瓣
2	鹽	1/8 小匙
	熱水、花生醬	各 1 杯
	酸子汁、椰子糖	各 3 大匙

1	4	chili peppers
	6	garlic cloves
2	1/8 t.	salt
	1 c. ea.:	hot water, peanut butter
	3 T. ea.:	tamarind juice, palm sugar

將 1 料搗碎或攪碎再拌入 2 料即成。此醬用法頗廣，可用以淋 *爪哇沙拉* (見74頁)，也可沾 *烤魚餅* (見34頁)、*玉米蝦餅* (見65頁)或各種沙爹等。

Grind 1 with a mortar and pestle or blender; add 2 and mix well. This sauce may be used to drizzle on *Java Salad* (p.75) or as a dipping sauce for *Fish Cakes in Banana Leaves* (p.35), *Corn & Shrimp Fritters* (p.65), or a variety of Sate dishes.

辛香醬泥
SPICE PASTES

炒香"辛香醬泥"是烹飪過程中很重要的步驟,為免炒焦,炒時可將辛香醬泥與油同時放入鍋內再開火,利用油溫慢慢提昇的同時炒到香味溢出,即可緊接拌入肉類或蔬菜一起烹調。

Stir-frying spice paste is an important step in preparing dishes. To prevent burning, place the paste and cooking oil into the unheated frying pan before turning on the stove. Gradually increase the degree of heat and stir-fry until fragrant; add meat or vegetable and continue stirring until done.

南洋菜的烹調過程中常用到辣椒、紅蔥頭、蒜頭、薑、南薑及蝦米等辛香料,由於加入這些辛香料,使菜餚產生獨特的南洋風味。有些菜餚在烹調前需先將辛香料攪成醬泥後,放入油內炒香再拌入肉類或蔬菜一起烹調,如此其濃郁的香味才會溶入湯汁內且不會有顆粒狀。辛香醬泥有時僅用單種,有時則使用多種辛香料混合做成,準備時可僅做一次烹調的份量,也可做多量再以小量分批包裝冰凍儲存。

When preparing Southeast Asian dishes, flavoring agents such as chili peppers, shallots, garlic, ginger root, galangal, and dried shrimp are used. These various spices and flavors characterize this unique cuisine. Some dishes call for grinding spices into paste then stir-frying the pastes in oil before adding other ingredients such as meat or vegetables. The pastes blend well into broths and sauces, as opposed to chopped bits and pieces. Sometimes a single type of spice paste is used, while other times a mixture of many spice pastes may be used. One may prepare spice pastes for one-time use; or if large quantities are prepared, they may be divided into small quantities and individually refrigerated for future use.

單種辛香醬泥
SINGLE SPICE PASTES

常用的有辣椒、紅蔥頭、蒜頭、薑、南薑及蝦米等,本書內稱為辣椒泥、紅蔥頭泥、蒜泥、薑泥、南薑泥及蝦米泥。

Most commonly used ingredients to grind into a paste are chili peppers, shallots, garlic, ginger, and dried shrimp. This cookbook refers to ground fresh chilies, ground shallots, ground fresh garlic, ground ginger root, ground fresh galangal, and ground dried shrimp.

辣椒泥	紅蔥頭泥	蒜泥	薑泥	南薑泥	蝦米泥
ground fresh chilies	ground shallots	ground fresh garlic	ground ginger root	ground galangal	ground dried shrimp

混合辛香醬泥
ASSORTED SPICE PASTES

本書內常用的混合辛香醬泥有四種。為了方便初學者，特訂出下面份量及組合以供參考，依照下面份量攪碎成醬泥後約可做成 1 杯 – 1 1/2 杯。

This cookbook contains four types of combined spice pastes. Novice cooks will find these recipes helpful. Each one makes about 1 - 1 1/2 cups of blended paste.

基本辣醬泥
辣椒	6 兩 (225 公克)
紅蔥頭、蒜頭	各 1 兩 (37.5 公克)

BASIC CHILI PASTE
1/2 lb. (225g)	chili peppers
1 1/4 oz. (37.5g) each:	shallots, garlic cloves

臘仁辣醬泥
辣椒	6 兩 (225 公克)
紅蔥頭、蒜頭	各 1 兩 (37.5 公克)
臘仁	1 兩 (37.5 公克)

CANDLENUT CHILI PASTE
1/2 lb. (225g)	chili peppers
1 1/4 oz. (37.5g) each:	shallots, garlic cloves
1 1/4 oz. (37.5g)	candlenuts

綜合辣醬泥
辣椒	6 兩 (225 公克)
紅蔥頭、臘仁	各 1 兩 (37.5 公克)
南薑、薑	各 1 兩 (37.5 公克)
蒜頭	1 兩 (37.5 公克)
黃薑粉	1 1/2 小匙

(以上攪碎成泥後才加入拌勻)

MIXED CHILI PASTE
1/2 lb. (225g)	chili peppers
1 1/4 oz. (37.5g) each:	shallots, candlenuts
1 1/4 oz. (37.5g) each:	galangal, ginger root
1 1/4 oz. (37.5g)	garlic cloves
1 1/2 t.	turmeric powder

(mix with the ground ingredients listed above)

蔥蒜醬泥
紅蔥頭	6 兩 (225 公克)
薑	1 兩 (37.5 公克)
蒜頭	1 兩 (37.5 公克)
臘仁	1 兩 (37.5 公克)

FRAGRANT PASTE
1/2 lb. (225g)	shallots
1 1/4 oz. (37.5g)	ginger root
1 1/4 oz. (37.5g)	garlic cloves
1 1/4 oz. (37.5g)	candlenuts

辛香醬泥的作法：

把選擇的單種或混合的辛香料略切小塊以方便搗碎，再用傳統的"杵"和"臼"搗碎，或以"攪碎機"攪碎成醬泥即可。當有多種辛香料需攪碎時，其順序應由最堅硬的先攪，再依序加入其他的材料，攪碎時若太乾可加少許油。

TO MAKE SPICE PASTES：

Whether using single or combined spices, cut all the ingredients into small pieces to make grinding easier. Use traditional mortar and pestle or blender to grind all the ingredients into a paste. When combining spices, mash and blend the hardest ingredients first, then add the other ingredients. If the consistency is too dry during grinding, add a little bit of oil to moisten.

海南雞飯 — Hainan Chicken Rice *(Nasi Ayam)*

雞	2斤4兩（1350公克）
① 薑（拍扁）	1塊
蔥	1支
蒜頭（拍扁）	6個
麻油	2大匙
② 米（洗淨瀝乾）	2杯
油	2大匙
雞高湯	2杯
香蘭葉	6片
③ 薑泥	1大匙
辣椒泥、醬油	各2大匙
醋、糖	各1小匙
鹽	⅛小匙
④ 黃瓜（切片）	1條
番茄（切片）	2個
芫荽葉	4大匙

< 4 人份 >

1 雞洗淨拭乾，以1½大匙鹽塗抹雞身內外，將①料塞入雞肚內，醃過夜。

2 水10杯燒開，放入雞水宜蓋滿雞身，大火燒開，改小火蓋鍋煮25分鐘熄火，燜5分鐘至雞熟，隨即將雞撈出，放入多量冰水內浸泡5分鐘（主要是使雞皮結實有彈性）。

3 雞撈出抹上2大匙麻油，待完全冷卻後切塊，雞湯除去浮在湯面的油脂，留2杯煮飯用。

4 將②料用電鍋煮成飯盛出，上擺雞塊以拌勻的③料當沾料，與④料配食。

■ 剩下的高湯可隨意加冬瓜或包心菜做成菜湯，連同做好的海南雞飯一起上桌，可說是典型星加坡菜。

Hainan Chicken Rice *(Nasi Ayam)*

< SERVES 4 >

3 lbs. (1350g) chicken	
① 1 piece ginger, crushed	
1 green onion	
6 garlic cloves, crushed	
2 T. sesame oil	
② 2 c. rice (washed and drained)	
2 T. oil	
2 c. chicken stock (reserved in step 3)	
6 pandan leaves	
③ 1 T. ground ginger root	
2 T. ea.: ground fresh chilies, soy sauce	
1 t. ea.: vinegar, sugar	
⅛ t. salt	
④ 1 cucumber, sliced	
2 tomatoes, sliced	
4 T. cilantro	

1 Wash chicken and pat dry. Rub 1½ T. salt inside and outside chicken. Place ① inside stomach; let set overnight.

2 Bring 10 c. of water to boil. Immerse chicken completely in water and bring to boil again over high heat. Reduce heat to low; cover and cook 25 minutes, turn off heat and let set for 5 minutes. Remove chicken and immediately immerse completely in ice water for 5 minutes to firm the meat and make the skin resilient.

3 Remove chicken and rub it with 2 T. of sesame oil. Allow chicken to cool completely; cut into pieces. Skim oil from the chicken stock; reserve two cups of stock.

4 Place ② in electric rice cooker* and cook. Remove rice to serving dish and place chicken pieces on top; mix ③ as dipping sauce and serve with ④.

* If rice cooker is not available, bring ② to boil over medium heat; reduce heat to low, cover and simmer for 20 minutes. Turn off heat and let stand for 10 minutes.

■ Vegetables (cabbage, winter squash) may be added to the remaining stock to make an invigorating and flavorful soup to be served with the Hainan Chicken Rice dish. This traditional dish is one of the most famous and popular meals in Singapore.

肉骨茶

Spiced Sparerib Soup *(Bak Kut Teh)*

< 4 人份 >

	小排骨	12兩（450公克）
①	白胡椒、鹽	各½ 小匙
②	蒜頭（拍扁）	2個
	豆醬（圖1）	1小匙
	糖	1大匙
	八角*	3顆
	丁香	6粒
	肉桂（2.5公分）	1支
③	甘草	3片
	白胡椒粒、鹽	各1小匙
	深色醬油	3大匙
	水	8杯

1 小排骨切塊，以①料醃½小時，油燒
熱大火將小排骨兩面煎黃鏟出。

2 油2大匙燒熱，小火炒香②料，約30秒
鐘使糖溶化後，放回煎好的排骨拌炒
均勻，加入③料燒開，改小火煮1至1
½小時至排骨熟軟，除去浮在湯面的
油脂即可。

* 八角形的香料，中馬結合的菜餚中，
常用此來調味。

■ 肉骨茶在南洋是很有名的養生美食，
煮一大鍋肉骨茶即可與白飯及油條配
食當餐。在當地的路邊攤或講究的餐
廳都有賣肉骨茶，除以小排骨為主料
外，有的還加香菇、豬內臟、當歸、
熟地、黨參或其他藥膳以增加特殊風
味，做為吸引顧客的號召。

< SERVES 4 >

	1 lb. (450g) pork spareribs
①	½ t. ea.: white pepper, salt
	2 garlic cloves, crushed
②	1 t. preserved soybeans (Fig.1)
	1 T. sugar
	3 star anise*
	6 cloves
	1 cinnamon stick, 1" (2.5cm) long
③	3 pieces licorice**
	1 t. ea.: white peppercorns, salt
	3 T. dark soy sauce
	8 c. water

1 Cut spareribs into bite size pieces. Mix with ①, let stand for
30 minutes. Heat oil and pan-fry ribs until golden brown.

2 Heat 2 T. oil; stir-fry ② over low heat for 30 seconds or
until fragrant and sugar has melted. Add spareribs and mix
well; add ③ and bring to boil. Reduce heat to low and cook
for 1½ hours until ribs are tender. Skim oil from soup surface. Serve.

* Star anise is used as the major seasoning in Chinese-
Malaysian cuisine and can be purchased in Asian markets.

** Licorice is a dried root used to enhance flavor and can be
purchased in Asian markets.

■ This dish is very popular in Southeast Asia as a health
food supplement. It can be found in fine restaurants or
among food stand street vendors. Pork liver, Chinese black
mushrooms and various seasonings and herbs (tangkuei,
cooked rehmannia and codonopsis), can be added to
enhance the health characteristics and flavor. May be
eaten with rice or crispy Chinese Crullers (you tiau).

1

南洋薄餅

< 4 人份 >

①	沙葛*（圖1）	切絲12兩（450公克）
	胡蘿蔔、四季豆	切絲各1杯
②	瘦絞肉	6兩（225公克）
	蝦仁（剁碎）	6兩（225公克）
	豆腐（炸黃、切絲）	1杯
③	蒜泥	1大匙
	豆醬（圖2）	2大匙
	深色醬油	1小匙
	鹽	1½ 小匙
	糖	4大匙
④	蛋皮絲**、黃瓜（去皮切絲）	各1杯
	蒜頭酥、碎花生（見15頁）	各¼ 杯
	辣椒絲	¼ 杯
	芫荽葉	½ 杯
	海鮮醬	½ 杯
	薄餅皮（春捲皮）	20張
	生菜葉	10片

1　將④料備好盛盤。③料內的豆醬壓成泥。

2　油4大匙燒熱，炒香③料，盛出一半備用。依序將①料放入鍋內，與鍋內餘醬以中火炒至喜歡的熟度撈出盛盤，餘汁不要。

3　將另一半醬，倒回鍋中，依序加入②料，炒至肉熟盛於盤上。

4　把所有的材料擺於桌上，取一片薄餅皮，上置半片生菜葉，依喜好放入備好的材料，在餅皮之邊緣抹上海鮮醬，包成春捲。

*　沙葛與蕃薯同屬莖科類，但沙葛含有大量的水份，味清甜，是薄餅的主要材料，沙葛也可當沙拉的材料生吃。

**　兩顆蛋打散，鍋面塗少許油，將蛋煎成蛋皮，取出切絲。

■　薄餅在不同地方取名不同，有的稱潤餅，這種餅在中國沿海一帶或有潮州人移民的地方，如台灣、南洋各地都很盛行。包在薄餅內的材料也因地方及喜好不同有所變化。將各種材料準備好擺在餐桌上，大家圍坐，邊包邊吃樂趣無窮。

Hokkienese Spring Rolls (Po Phia)

< SERVES 4 >

①	1 lb. (450g) jicama* (Fig.1), shredded	
	1 c. ea. (shredded): carrots, string beans	
②	½ lb. (225g) lean ground pork	
	½ lb. (225g) shelled shrimp, minced	
	1 c. regular tofu (fried, shredded)	
③	1 T. ground fresh garlic	
	2 T. preserved soybeans (Fig.2)	
	1 t. dark soy sauce	
	1½ t. salt	
	4 T. sugar	
④	1 c. ea. (shredded): egg sheet**, peeled cucumber	
	¼ c. ea.: crispy garlic, ground roasted peanuts (p.15), shredded chili peppers	
	½ c. cilantro	
	½ c. hoisin sauce	
	20 ready-made egg roll skins	
	10 green lettuce leaves	

1　Prepare ingredients in ④ and put in one dish. Mash preserved soybeans of ③ into paste.

2　Heat 4 T. oil; stir-fry ③ until fragrant. Remove half the sauce and reserve. Sequentially, add ① in the sauce; cook over medium heat to desired texture. Drain and discard juice; place the mixture in a second dish.

3　Return the reserved sauce and sequentially add ②; stir-fry until meat is cooked. Remove and put in another dish.

4　Place all three dishes on the table. Put ½ of a lettuce leaf on an egg roll skin and add on ingredients from the three dishes as desired. Roll up the spring roll, coating the edge of the egg roll skin with hoisin sauce to help seal the roll.

*　Jicama and yam belong to the same category, but jicama contains more water with a sweeter flavor and can be eaten raw in a salad.

**　Lightly beat 2 eggs. Coat a pan with a little oil. Pour in eggs and rotate the pan to create thin egg sheet.

■　Another very popular dish, which originated along the Eastern coastline of China and spread throughout Southeast Asia. The fun part of eating this meal is that the various ingredients are placed on the table, and the diners select and prepare their own meal to their personal taste.

1

2

蝦麵

<　2人份　>

	熟油麵*(圖1)	12兩(450公克)
①	空心菜、綠豆芽	各½ 杯
	蝦仁 12隻，魚餅**(圖2)12片	
	海鮮高湯	5杯
②	鹽 1小匙，糖 ½ 小匙	
	醬油	2大匙
	青蔥末、辣椒絲	各1大匙
③	油蔥酥、培根酥	各1大匙
	胡椒	1小匙

1　多量水燒開，將①料及熟麵分別川燙，再將蝦仁燙熟，依序盛於2個麵碗內，再擺上魚餅。

2　將②料燒開，隨即倒入麵碗內，最後撒上③料，可當早餐、正餐或宵夜。

*　可到市場買現成的，或用一般乾麵4兩(150公克)煮熟，取代油麵12兩。

**　魚餅是以魚漿、蛋及太白粉做成，可買現成。

■　蝦麵其獨特之處乃湯汁鮮美。原始作法是在③料內加了炸豬肥油渣，為方便讀者，改以培根酥取代。

星式喇沙

<　2人份　>

	乾米粉*(圖3)	4兩(150公克)
	綠豆芽 ½ 杯，帶殼中蝦 8隻	
①	魚餅(圖2)	12片
	水煮蛋(去殼、切半)	2個
	臘仁辣醬泥(見19頁)	4大匙
②	薑泥、蝦醬、蝦米泥	各1小匙
	香茅(拍扁) 1支，南薑 2片	
	高湯 4杯，鹽 2小匙	
	豆腐泡**(圖4)	12個
	濃椰奶	1杯
③	辣椒絲、油蔥酥	各1大匙
	芫荽菜	1大匙

1　多量水燒開，分別將豆芽及米粉川燙，再將蝦燙熟，依序盛於2個麵碗內，再擺上①料。

2　將②料燒開加豆腐泡及濃椰奶再燒開，倒入麵碗內，撒上③料即成。

*　乾米粉需泡水，米粉4兩(150公克)煮熟可得12兩(450公克)。

**　豆腐泡又稱小豆泡，也可用豆腐炸成表面金黃取代。

■　喇沙香濃可口，是結合了中、馬的口味的道地點心，也可當正餐。

1

2

Prawn Noodle Soup *(Hae Mee)*

< SERVES 2 >

1 lb. (450g) boiled yellow
   noodles* (Fig.1)

1
- ½ c. water spinach
- ½ c. bean sprouts
- 12 shelled shrimp
- 12 fish cakes** (Fig.2)

2
- 5 c. seafood stock
- 1 t. salt
- ½ t. sugar
- 2 T. soy sauce

3
- 1 T. minced green onion
- 1 T. shredded chili peppers
- 1 T. crispy shallots (p.15)
- 1 T. bacon bits
- 1 t. pepper

1. Bring a pot of water to boil. Blanch ① and noodles separately; place in two bowls. Cook shrimp in boiling water. Remove from pot and place in the bowls. Place six fish cakes in each bowl.

2. Bring ② to boil and pour equally into the two bowls. Sprinkle on ③. This dish makes a very appetizing meal or snack.

* Buy ready-boiled noodles or cook ⅓ lb. (150g) of dry noodles as a substitute for 1 lb. (450g) of boiled yellow noodles.

** Use ready-made fish cakes or combine fish paste, eggs and cornstarch to make fish cakes.

■ This popular dish is "special" due to the uniqueness of the soup. Originally, rather than using bacon bits, the fatty part of the pork was chopped and deep-fried to enhance the flavor of the soup.

Noodles in Spicy Coconut Milk Soup *(Laksa Lemak)*

< SERVES 2 >

⅓ lb. (150g) rice sticks* (Fig.3)

½ c. bean sprouts

8 medium shrimp

1
- 12 fish cakes (Fig.2)
- 2 hard-boiled eggs
  (shelled, cut in half)

2
- 4 T. candlenut chili paste (p.19)
- 1 t. ground ginger root
- 1 t. shrimp paste (p.11)
- 1 t. ground dried shrimp
- 1 lemon grass, crushed
- 2 galangal slices
- 4 c. stock, 2 t. salt

12 tofu-puff** (Fig.4)

1 c. thick coconut milk

3
- 1 T. crispy shallots (p.15)
- 1 T. cilantro
- 1 T. shredded chili peppers

1. Boil a pot of water. Blanch bean sprouts and rice sticks separately; place in two bowls. Cook shrimp in boiling water. Remove from pot and place in two separate bowls. Place an equal portion of ① in each bowl.

2. Bring ② to boil; add fried tofu and coconut milk; bring to boil again. Divide into each bowl. Sprinkle on ③; serve.

* Soften rice sticks by soaking in water. After boiling ⅓ lb. (150g) of rice sticks will expand to 1 lb. (450g).

** Ready-made fried tofu may be substituted by deep-frying fresh regular tofu to golden brown.

■ Laksa is a very delicious dish which combines the Chinese and Malaysian flavors. Can be served as a snack or main meal.

3

4

洋蔥雞塊

< 2 人份 >

	雞腿	1斤(600公克)
[1]	鹽、糖	各1小匙
	甜醬油	2大匙
	青檸檬汁	1大匙
	洋蔥絲	1杯
[2]	辣椒絲	½ 杯
	胡椒	1小匙

1 雞腿洗淨拭乾，切塊，以[1]料醃2小時。

2 油3大匙燒熱，炒香洋蔥絲，加入雞塊炒至雞肉變色，隨即加水 ½ 杯燒開，改小火蓋鍋燜煮25分鐘，加[2]料炒拌即可。

香汁烤雞

< 2 人份 >

	雞腿	1斤(600公克)
[1]	鹽、青檸檬汁	各1小匙
	綜合辣醬泥(見19頁)	5大匙
[2]	香茅(切薄片)	1支
	檸檬葉(切細絲)	3片
	椰奶	1杯
[3]	鹽	½ 小匙
	酸子汁	½ 大匙

1 雞腿洗淨拭乾，以[1]料及2大匙的綜合辣醬泥醃1小時，置於烤盤。

2 烤箱預熱230℃(450°F)，以上火將醃好的雞腿(雞皮朝上)烤10分鐘至表面呈金黃色。

3 油3大匙燒熱，炒香剩下的3大匙綜合辣醬泥及[2]料，再加入[3]料及烤香的雞腿，以大火燒開，改小火蓋鍋燜煮20分鐘(中途需翻動)至雞肉熟即可。

■ 這道菜中的雞是先烤過之後再煮，所以擁有烤的香味也融入了煮的湯汁於其中，是道濃郁深具馬來風味的菜。

Chicken with Onions *(Ayam Tempra)*

< SERVES 2 >

	1⅓ lbs. (600g) chicken legs
[1]	1 t. ea.: salt, sugar
	2 T. sweet soy sauce
	1 T. lime juice
	1 c. shredded onions
[2]	½ c. shredded chili peppers
	1 t. pepper

1 Wash chicken legs and pat dry; cut into pieces. Mix with [1] and let stand for 2 hours.

2 Heat 3 T. oil; stir-fry onions until aromatic. Add in chicken pieces and stir-fry until color changes; add ½ c. water and bring to boil. Reduce heat to low, cover and cook 25 minutes. Add [2], mix well and serve.

Fragrant Coconut Chicken *(Ayam Kleo)*

< SERVES 2 >

	1⅓ lbs. (600g) chicken legs
[1]	1 t. ea.: salt, lime juice
	5 T. mixed chili paste (p.19)
[2]	1 lemon grass, sliced
	3 kaffir leaves, shredded
	1 c. coconut milk
[3]	½ t. salt
	½ T. tamarind juice

1 Wash chicken legs and pat dry; rub with [1] and 2 T. mixed chili paste; let stand for 1 hour. Place on a baking pan.

2 Preheat oven to 450°F (230°C). Bake chicken, skin side up, for 10 minutes or until golden brown. Remove from oven.

3 Heat 3 T. oil; stir-fry remaining 3 T. mixed chili paste and [2] until aromatic. Add [3] and chicken legs; bring to boil over high heat. Reduce heat to low; cover and cook 20 minutes (turn chicken occasionally) until cooked through.

■ Chicken is first baked and then cooked to enhance the flavor and aroma of the sauce. This is a very delicious, Malaysian family dish enjoyed throughout Southeast Asia.

五香肉捲

< 4 人份 >

①	豬絞肉	6兩 (225公克)
	蝦仁	4兩 (150公克)
	荸薺	½ 杯
	蛋	1個
②	鹽、深色醬油	各½ 小匙
	玉米粉	½ 小匙
	糖、醬油、五香粉*	各1小匙
	麻油	1大匙
	新鮮豆腐皮 (16公分四方)	4片
	炸油	2杯

1 將①料內的蝦剁成泥、荸薺剁碎。

2 蛋打散與①、②料混合仔細攪拌成餡，分成4份。

3 豆腐皮攤開，取1份肉餡置於腐皮前端(圖1)，包成春捲形狀，皮邊用水沾黏，以大火蒸10分鐘或微波爐加熱8分鐘至肉餡熟備用。

4 炸油燒熱，以中火將肉捲炸3分鐘至金黃色，使外皮酥脆。切片擺盤。

* 以八角、肉桂、丁香、茴香子及花椒混合磨成粉狀。

■ 肉捲可用來當自助餐用的菜餚、前菜、或當配飯菜等多種用途。

1

Five-Spice Meat Rolls *(Goh Heong)*

< SERVES 4 >

1 | ½ lb. (225g) ground pork
   | ⅓ lb. (150g) shelled shrimp
   | ½ c. water chestnuts

   1 egg

2 | ½ t. ea.: salt, dark soy sauce,
   | cornstarch
   | 1 t. ea.: sugar, soy sauce,
   | five-spice powder*
   | 1 T. sesame oil

   4 fresh bean curd sheets,
        6½"x 6½" (16cm x 16cm)

   2 c. oil for deep-frying

1   Chop shrimp and mash into a paste; chop water chestnuts.

2   Beat egg and then add ① and ②; mix well. Divide into four portions.

3   Place each portion on one side of a bean curd sheet (Fig.1). Roll up to make a "Spring Egg Roll". Moisten edges with water to seal. Steam over high heat for 10 minutes, or microwave for 8 minutes until cooked.

4   Heat oil, deep-fry meat roll over medium heat for 3 minutes until golden brown and crispy. Cut into pieces and serve.

*   Five-spice powder is made by combining star anise, cinnamon, cloves, cumin and pepper and grinding into a fine powder.

■   This may be eaten as an appetizer or main dish. Great to take to a potluck meal.

Fried Tamarind Chicken *(Ayam Goreng Asam)*

< SERVES 2 >

   1⅓ lbs. (600g) chicken legs,
        cut in pieces

1 | 3 T. tamarind juice
   | 2 t. sugar
   | 1½ T. soy sauce
   | ½ t. ea.: salt, pepper

   2 c. oil for deep-frying

1   Wash chicken and pat dry. Mix with ①; let stand for 2 hours.

2   Heat oil; pat chicken dry and deep-fry over medium heat for 8 minutes until golden brown. Remove and drain. Dip in "Shrimp Paste Sambal" (p.16), if desired. May also be served with cucumber and tomato slices according to personal preference.

■   Another popular Nyonya dish, flavor-enhanced by the tamarind juice used for marinating. Tamarind is abundant in Southeast Asia and used extensively in cooking to enhance the appetite.

炸酸子雞

< 2 人 份 >

   雞腿(切塊)   1斤(600公克)

1 | 酸子汁   3大匙
   | 糖   2小匙
   | 醬油   1½ 大匙
   | 鹽、胡椒   各½ 小匙
   | 炸油   2杯

1   雞塊洗淨拭乾，以①料醃2小時。

2   炸油燒熱，將雞塊拭乾，用中火炸8分鐘至雞肉熟且呈褐色，撈出瀝乾油，食時可沾"蝦醬味辣醬"（見16頁），並配黃瓜及番茄。

■   利用南洋盛產的酸子汁，來醃雞肉，炸出來的雞味道特別不一樣，帶有酸味且顏色偏黑，當地人常用酸子來炸魚或其他肉類以增加食慾。

南洋滷鴨

<　6 人份　>

鴨		3斤(1800公克)
①	五香粉* 2大匙，鹽 1小匙	
②	蒜頭、紅蔥頭　(拍扁)各5個	
	八角** 3朵，　薑 4片	
	黃薑粉	½ 小匙
	香茅(拍扁)	2支
	醬油、深色醬油　各½ 杯	
	糖 6大匙，鹽 ½ 小匙	
	水	8杯

1 鴨去除肥油，洗淨拭乾，以①料抹勻鴨身內外，醃過夜。

2 將②料燒開放入鴨，水蓋過鴨身八分滿，再燒開改中火蓋鍋煮1至1½小時至喜歡的熟軟度撈出(中途需翻面)，待涼後剁塊。配飯或粥皆適宜。

* 以八角、肉桂、丁香、茴香子及花椒混合磨成粉狀。

** 八角形的香料，中馬結合的菜餚中，常用此來調味。

■ 煮過鴨的滷汁可滷蛋、豆干或內臟類。

娘惹滷肉

<　4 人份　>

五花肉(圖1)		1斤(600公克)
深色醬油		1大匙
香菇(泡軟)		6朵
①	紅蔥頭泥、芫荽子粉　各2大匙	
	蒜泥	1大匙
	豆醬(圖2)	1½ 大匙
	肉桂(2.5公分)	1支
②	醬油、深色醬油　各1大匙	
	糖、胡椒	各1大匙
	鹽 ¼ 小匙，水 1杯	

1 將①料內的豆醬壓成泥。五花肉切塊，以深色醬油醃1小時，油2大匙燒熱，將肉塊煎至表面呈金黃色撈出，餘油不要。

2 油1大匙燒熱，炒香①料後加入肉塊、香菇及②料燒開，改小火蓋鍋燜煮1至1½小時至汁濃肉熟軟即成。

■ 肉可不煎而直接放入①、②料燒煮，或用日本味噌取代豆醬來變化，此菜餚香濃可口，頗得家父青睞。

Savory Spiced Duck *(Bebek Hong)*

< SERVES 6 >

4 lbs. (1800g) whole duck

[1]
- 2 T. five-spice powder*
- 1 t. salt

[2]
- 5 garlic cloves, crushed
- 5 shallots, crushed
- 3 star anises**
- 4 ginger slices
- ½ t. turmeric powder
- 2 lemon grass, crushed
- ½ c. soy sauce
- ½ c. dark soy sauce
- 6 T. sugar
- ½ t. salt
- 8 c. water

1　Remove fat from duck; wash and pat dry. Rub [1] inside and outside of duck, let set overnight.

2　Bring [2] to boil; immerse duck to 80% covered. Bring to boil again; reduce heat to medium. Cover and cook 1 to 1½ hours (must turn occasionally), until desired tenderness is reached. Remove and let cool. Cut the duck into pieces; let cool. Serve with rice or rice porridge.

*　Five-spice powder is made by combining star anise, cinnamon, cloves, cumin and pepper and grinding into a fine powder.

**　Star anise is used as the major seasoning in Chinese-Malaysian cuisine.

■　Preserved tofu or hard-boiled eggs may be added to the remaining sauce in which the duck was cooked.

Nyonya Pork Stew *(Babi Hong)*

< SERVES 4 >

1⅓ lbs. (600g) fresh bacon (Fig.1)

1 T. dark soy sauce

6 pre-softened Chinese black mushrooms

[1]
- 2 T. ea.: ground shallots, coriander powder
- 1 T. ground fresh garlic
- 1½ T. preserved soybeans (Fig.2)
- 1 cinnamon stick, 1" (2.5cm) long

[2]
- 1 T. ea.: soy sauce, dark soy sauce, sugar , pepper
- ¼ t. salt
- 1 c. water

1　Mash preserved soybeans in [1] into paste. Cut bacon into pieces; mix with the dark soy sauce; let stand for 1 hour. Heat 2 T. oil, pan-fry bacon until golden brown. Remove bacon and discard oil.

2　Heat 1 T. oil; stir-fry [1] until fragrant. Add in bacon pieces, mushrooms and [2]; bring to boil. Reduce heat to low, cover and cook 1 to 1½ hours until sauce is thick and meat is tender. Serve.

■　As an option and to simplify the procedures, the bacon may be cooked directly with ingredients [1] & [2] without pan-frying, or Japanese miso may be used as a substitute for preserved soybeans of [1].

1

2

香醋炸魚

< 4 人份 >

魚排		12兩(450公克)
1	鹽、青檸檬汁	各½ 小匙
	炸油	2杯
2	薑絲	1大匙
	臘仁辣醬泥(見19頁)	5大匙
	黃薑粉	½ 小匙
3	水 ¼ 杯，鹽 ½ 小匙	
	糖 1½ 大匙，醋 2大匙	
	青、紅辣椒絲	2大匙

1 魚洗淨抹乾，以1料醃1小時，再拭乾水份。

2 炸油燒熱將魚大火炸6分鐘至剛熟，表面呈金黃色備用。

3 油3大匙燒熱，將2料炒香，隨入3料及魚翻拌煮至汁略收乾，撒入辣椒絲即起鍋。

■ 我姨婆曾是烹飪老師，她所做過的菜均留給我深刻印象，此為她拿手菜之一。

烤魚餅

< 20 條 >

魚漿*(圖1)		12兩(450公克)
1	濃椰奶	½ 杯
	蛋白(打散)	2個
	胡椒、南薑汁	各1小匙
	糖、太白粉	各2小匙
香蕉葉(10公分x16公分)		20片

1 將1料放入魚漿內，用力攪拌。

2 香蕉葉攤開，取1½大匙的魚漿置於中間，捲成長扁狀，兩端以牙籤固定成魚餅。

3 烤箱預熱230℃(450℉)，將魚餅放入烤15分鐘，若用烤架，則每面烤15分鐘。可配飯、當前菜或零食。隨喜好沾"花生辣醬"(見17頁)。

* 魚漿因廠牌不同而鹹淡不一，需視情況加鹽。

Fried Fish with Vinaigrette Sauce *(Ikan Achar)*

< SERVES 4 >

1 lb. (450g) fish fillet

1. ½ t. ea.: salt, lime juice

2 c. oil for deep-frying

2.
- 1 T. shredded ginger
- 5 T. candlenut chili paste (p.19)
- ½ t. turmeric powder

3.
- ¼ c. water
- ½ t. salt
- 1½ T. sugar
- 2 T. vinegar

2 T. shredded chili peppers
(green and red)

1 Wash fish and pat dry. Marinate in 1 for 1 hour; pat dry again.

2 Heat oil; deep-fry fish over high heat for 6 minutes until just cooked and golden brown.

3 Heat 3 T. oil; stir-fry 2 until fragrant. Add 3 and the fish. Cook until liquid is almost evaporated. Sprinkle on chili peppers and serve.

■ My grandmother's sister was a cooking teacher. This is one of her many favorites that she enjoyed cooking. I have many pleasurable memories of this delicious dish.

1

Fish Cakes in Banana Leaves *(Otak-Otak Ikan)*

< MAKES 20 >

1 lb. (450g) fish paste* (Fig.1)

1.
- ½ c. thick coconut milk
- 2 egg whites, lightly beaten
- 1 t. ea.: pepper, galangal juice
- 2 t. ea.: sugar, cornstarch

20 banana leaves, 4" x 6 ⅜"
(10cm x 16cm)

1 Mix fish paste with 1 thoroughly, until there is a smooth and sticky mixture.

2 Place 1½ T. of mixture in the center of a banana leaf. Roll up and insert a toothpick in each end to close to create fish cakes.

3 Pre-heat oven to 450°F (230°C); bake the fish cakes for 15 minutes. If an open grill is used, cook each side 15 minutes. Serve with rice as a main dish. It can also be served as an appetizer or snack. Best eaten when dipped in "Peanut Sambal" (p.17).

* Different brands of fish paste have different flavors, some are more salty than others. Choose to your personal preference.

娘惹蒸魚

< 2 人份 >

	魚	1斤(600公克)
①	鹽、胡椒	各¼ 小匙
②	薑絲、鹹菜	各1½ 大匙
	香菇絲	1½ 大匙
③	醬油	1½ 大匙
	糖、麻油	各⅔ 小匙
	高湯(或水)	⅓ 杯
④	芫荽葉	½ 大匙
	辣椒絲、青蔥絲	各½ 大匙

1 魚洗淨拭乾,以①料塗抹魚身。

2 盤底先抹油½大匙,將魚置其上,撒上②料,再淋上拌勻的③料,大火蒸8分鐘至魚熟或用微波爐加熱5分鐘,最後撒上④料再加熱1分鐘即成。

■ 味道鮮美的娘惹蒸魚為家父所鍾愛,我每次回家必親自烹煮與他老人家共享。

辣醬螃蟹

< 2 人份 >

	螃蟹	1½ 斤(900公克)
①	薑泥	½ 大匙
	蒜泥	1大匙
	辣椒泥	2大匙
	豆醬(圖1)	½ 大匙
②	水⅔ 杯,醬油 1大匙	
	糖、醋	各½ 大匙
	蛋(打散)	1個
	青蔥段	¼ 杯

1 螃蟹切成四大塊,蟹鉗搥破。①料內的豆醬壓成泥,免煮後有顆粒在汁內。

2 油3大匙燒熱,炒香①料,加入螃蟹翻炒均勻,續加入②料燒開,改中火蓋鍋燜煮10分鐘(中途需翻拌),再開大火,倒入蛋液及青蔥翻拌,起鍋前淋上1大匙油即成。

■ 當地人都用活蟹,是路邊攤常見的菜,當配飯菜外也是配啤酒的好伴侶。

辣醬龍蝦‧辣醬蛤蜊

用龍蝦或蛤蜊代替螃蟹,其他材料及作法同上。

1

Nyonya Steamed Fish (Ikan Kukus - Nyonya)

< SERVES 2 >

1⅓ lbs. (600g) fish

1 ¼ t. ea.: salt, pepper

2
1½ T. shredded ginger root
1½ T. pickled mustard
        cabbage
1½ T. shredded Chinese
        black mushrooms

3
1½ T. soy sauce
⅔ t. ea.: sugar, sesame oil
⅓ c. stock or water

4
½ T. cilantro
½ T. shredded green onion
½ T. shredded chili peppers

1   Wash fish and pat dry. Rub 1 on fish.

2   Coat a plate with ½ T. oil and place fish on the plate. Sprinkle ingredients 2 and then pour on mixture 3. Steam fish over high heat for 8 minutes or cook 5 minutes in a microwave. Sprinkle on 4 and cook again for 1 minute.

■   The distinction of this dish is the unique fresh flavor.

Spicy Crab (Kepiting Pedas)

< SERVES 2 >

2 lbs. (900g) crab

1
½ T. ground ginger root
1 T. ground fresh garlic
2 T. ground fresh chilies
½ T. preserved soybeans (Fig.1)

2
⅔ c. water
1 T. soy sauce
½ T. ea.: sugar, vinegar

1 egg, beaten
¼ c. sectioned green onions

1   Cut crab into 4 pieces. Crack the claw shells. Mash preserved soybeans in 1 thoroughly to prevent lumps in sauce after cooking.

2   Heat 3 T. oil; stir-fry 1 until fragrant. Add crab and mix well. Add 2 and bring to boil; reduce heat to medium, cover and cook 10 minutes stirring occasionally. Turn heat to high; pour in egg and green onions; mix well. Sprinkle 1 T. oil on top; remove immediately.

■   This dish is best when made from live crab and as a result, offers an unforgettable palate pleasing taste and is very popular in Singapore. It can be found everywhere from restaurants to street vendors, and is often enjoyed with beer.

Spicy Lobster · Spicy Clam
Use lobster or clams instead of crab, other ingredients and cooking procedures are the same as above.

椰汁蝦

< 2 人份 >

	蝦仁（留尾）	6兩（225公克）
	鳳梨丁	½ 杯
①	基本辣醬泥（見19頁）	3大匙
	黃薑粉	¼ 小匙
	蝦醬	½ 小匙
	香茅（拍扁）	1支
	檸檬葉	3片
②	鹽	½ 小匙
	糖	1小匙
	醋	½ 大匙
	椰奶	1杯
	辣椒（略切）	2支

1　油2大匙燒熱，先炒香①料再加入②料，煮開後加入蝦仁及鳳梨，翻炒數下，蝦仁轉紅色，即可加入辣椒拌炒起鍋。

■　非常容易學的一道馬來風味菜，湯汁濃郁具甜辣味，可淋在飯上食用。

酸辣鳳梨蝦仁

< 2 人份 >

	蝦（帶殼）	6兩（225公克）
	鳳梨丁	½ 杯
①	基本辣醬泥（見19頁）	3大匙
	蝦醬	1小匙
	鹽、糖	各1小匙
	酸子汁	2½ 大匙
	香茅（拍扁）	1支

1　將①料拌匀，加2杯水大火燒開，改小火煮3分鐘，加入蝦及鳳梨丁翻炒燒開，見蝦變色肉熟即起鍋。可撒些芫荽當盤飾。

■　此道菜酸辣開胃，較偏娘惹口味，湯汁淋在飯、麵或米粉上皆適宜。

Shrimp in Thick Coconut Gravy
(Udang Lemak)

< SERVES 2 >

	½ lb. (225g) shelled shrimp with tail intact
	½ c. diced pineapple
①	3 T. basic chili paste (p.19)
	¼ t. turmeric powder
	½ t. shrimp paste (p.11)
	1 lemon grass, crushed
	3 kaffir leaves
②	½ t. salt
	1 t. sugar
	½ T. vinegar
	1 c. coconut milk
	2 chili peppers, coarsely cut

1　Heat 2 T. oil; stir-fry ① until fragrant and add ②; bring to boil. Add shrimp and pineapple; mix and let boil. When shrimp is cooked and changes color, add chili peppers; mix well and remove.

■　This dish has a sweet and hot flavor that goes well with rice and is an easy to prepare Malaysian style dish.

Hot and Sour Pineapple Shrimp
(Udang Nanas Asam)

< SERVES 2 >

	½ lb. (225g) shrimp
	½ c. diced pineapple
①	3 T. basic chili paste (p.19)
	1 t. shrimp paste (p.11)
	1 t. ea.: salt, sugar
	2½ T. tamarind juice
	1 lemon grass, crushed

1　Mix ① and add 2 c. water; bring to boil. Reduce heat to low and cook 3 minutes. Add shrimp and pineapple; mix well and let boil until shrimp is cooked and changes color. Sprinkle with some cilantro as garnish.

■　This is a Nyonya style dish and acts as an appetite enhancer because of its hot and sour flavor. The sauce can be poured on noodles, rice and rice sticks.

蝦米炒空心菜

< 2 人 份 >

	空心菜	12兩（450公克）
①	基本辣醬泥（見19頁）	3大匙
	蝦米泥	1大匙
	蝦醬	½ 小匙
②	糖、醬油	各1小匙
	辣椒絲	1大匙

1　空心菜洗淨，瀝乾水份切段。

2　油3大匙燒熱，炒香①料，隨入空心菜及②料，以大火拌炒即可。

■　南洋盛產空心菜，是一道在當地的小吃攤或飯店都可以找到的大眾化菜餚。蝦醬在這道菜中扮演很重要的角色，不可缺少。

辣醬淋茄子

< 4 人 份 >

	茄子	12兩（450公克）
	炸油	適量
①	基本辣醬泥（見19頁）	4½ 大匙
	蝦醬	½ 小匙
	香茅（拍扁）	1支
②	糖	1½ 小匙
	鹽	¼ 小匙

1　茄子洗淨，拭乾後對半切開。

2　炸油燒熱，以中火將茄子炸4分鐘至熟軟呈金黃色，撈出瀝乾油，置盤備用。

3　油3大匙燒熱，炒香①料，再加入②料拌炒均勻，淋在炸好的茄子上。

■　用①及②料混合煮出來的醬汁非常可口下飯，是道眾所皆知的典型南洋家庭菜。

Spicy Kangkung with Dried Shrimp
(Kangkung Tumis)

< SERVES 2 >

1 lb. (450g) Kangkung (water spinach)	
3 T. basic chili paste (p.19)	
① **1 T. ground dried shrimp**	
½ t. shrimp paste (p.11)	
② **1 t. ea.: sugar, soy sauce**	
1 T. shredded chili peppers	

1　Wash and drain water spinach, cut into pieces.

2　Heat 3 T. oil; stir-fry ① until aromatic. Add water spinach and ②. Briefly stir-fry over high heat. Serve.

■　Water spinach is very plentiful in Southeast Asia and is often found in its cuisine. The shrimp paste is essential to the flavor of this very popular dish, served in the finest restaurants as well as by street vendors.

Spicy Garlic Sauce and Eggplant
(Sambal Terong)

< SERVES 4 >

1 lb. (450g) Asian eggplants	
oil for deep-frying	
4½ T. basic chili paste (p.19)	
① **½ t. shrimp paste (p.11)**	
1 lemon grass, crushed	
② **1½ t. sugar**	
¼ t. salt	

1　Wash eggplants and pat dry. Cut each in half, lengthwise.

2　Heat oil; deep-fry eggplants over medium heat for 4 minutes until cooked through and golden brown. Remove and drain; put on a plate.

3　Heat 3 T. oil, stir-fry ① until aromatic; add ② and mix well. Pour over eggplants and serve.

■　Combining ingredients ① & ②, makes a very delicious sauce that is traditionally served with family meals and is known all over Singapore.

木薯椰奶糕

<< 12 個 >>

①	木薯泥*（圖1）	12兩（450公克）
	椰子糖	4兩（150公克）
	糖 5大匙，鹽 ¼ 小匙	
	椰茸 ⅓ 杯，椰奶 ¼ 杯	
	香蕉葉（15公分四方）	12張

1　將①料放入容器內，攪拌均勻成木薯泥。

2　洗淨抹乾的蕉葉攤開，取1½大匙的木薯泥放在每片香蕉葉中間，左右兩邊對摺，上下兩端向內摺，全部做好放入蒸籠內，以大火蒸20分鐘。

*　木薯與蕃薯同屬莖科類，含有豐富的澱粉質，在南洋經常用木薯當主食或用來作糕點，在市面上可買到冷凍的木薯泥。

椰茸糯米球

<< 12 個 >>

	椰茸	1杯
	糯米粉	4兩（150公克）
①	鹽 ⅛ 小匙 ， 油 2大匙	
	香蘭葉精	¼ 小匙
	熱水	½ 杯
	椰子糖（壓碎）	½ 杯

1　椰茸拌入¼小匙的鹽，蒸15分鐘，或用微波爐加熱3分鐘備用。

2　糯米粉倒入容器內，加入拌勻的①料略攪拌後，揉成軟硬適中的麵糰。

3　麵糰分成12份，每份以手壓扁，中間放½小匙的椰子糖，包緊搓成圓球。

4　多量水燒開，將糯米球一次一個全部放入，煮開至糯米球浮出水面即熟，撈出放在椰茸上滾動，使沾滿椰茸即成。

■　這種點心在南洋各地很普遍，唯名稱各異。

Steamed Cassava Cake *(Lebat Ubi Kayu)*

<< MAKES 12 >>

①	1 lb. (450g) grated cassava* (Fig.1)
	⅓ lb. (150g) palm sugar
	5 T. sugar, ¼ t. salt
	⅓ c. shredded coconut, ¼ c. coconut milk
	12 banana leaves, 6" x 6" (15cm x 15cm)

1　Place ① in a container and mix well to create a paste.

2　Wash banana leaves and wipe dry. Place 1½ T. of cassava paste in the middle of each leaf. Fold over the left and right edges, then fold bottom and top edges over to cover the cassava paste. When folded, place all of them together in a steamer and steam over high heat for 20 minutes.

*　Cassava and yam are the same root category. Cassava has a very rich starch content and is served as a main meal in Southeast Asia. Also served in popular desserts. Frozen grated cassava can be purchased in most markets.

Sweet Coconut Rice Balls
(Kuih Buah Malaka)

<< MAKES 12 >>

	1 c. shredded coconut
	⅓ lb. (150g) glutinous rice powder
①	⅛ t. salt, 2 T. oil
	¼ t. pandan extract
	½ c. hot water
	½ c. palm sugar, crushed

1　Mix ¼ t. salt with shredded coconut and steam for 15 minutes or microwave at high for 3 minutes.

2　Put glutinous rice powder in a container and add mixture ①. Lightly mix and then knead to make a smooth dough.

3　Divide dough into 12 portions; flatten each portion to form a round of dough. In the middle of each, place ½ t. palm sugar and gather the edges to enclose the filling. Roll into a ball.

4　Boil a pot of water. Place one ball at a time in the boiling water until all are immersed. Bring to boil and cook until all balls float to the surface. Remove and roll in the shredded coconut. Serve.

■　This dessert is very popular in Southeast Asia under many and varied names.

1

香辣炒麵

< 2 人份 >

熟油麵＊(圖1)　12兩(450公克)

①

雞胸肉、炸豆腐
　　　　切條共6兩(225公克)
蝦仁　　　　　　　　　8隻

②

辣椒泥、蒜泥、醬油　各1大匙
深色醬油　　　　　　2大匙
蝦醬　　　　　　　　½ 小匙
鹽　¼ 小匙(口味淡者可省略)

包心菜(切絲)　　　　　1杯
綠豆芽　　　　　　　　½ 杯

③

芹菜葉(切絲)、芫荽葉各1大匙
辣椒(略切)　　　　　　1支
油蔥酥　　　　　　　2大匙

Aromatic Spicy Noodles *(Mee Goreng)*

< SERVES 2 >

1 lb. (450g) boiled yellow
  noodles* (Fig.1)

1
½ lb. (225g) total (cut in
  strips): boneless chicken
  breast, fried regular tofu
8 shelled shrimp

2
1 T. ground fresh chilies
1 T. ground fresh garlic
1 T. soy sauce
2 T. dark soy sauce
½ t. shrimp paste (p.11)
¼ t. salt, optional
1 c. shredded cabbage
½ c. bean sprouts

3
1 T. shredded celery leaves
1 T. cilantro
1 chili pepper, coarsely cut
2 T. crispy shallots (p.15)

1 Heat 3 T. oil. Add ① and stir-fry until chicken turns white and shrimp turns pink. Move mixture to the side of pan and stir-fry ② in center until fragrant; add cabbage and noodles, mixing all ingredients together. Add bean sprouts and stir-fry briefly.

2 Remove noodles to a plate. Sprinkle on ③ Serve.

* Pre-cooked yellow noodles may be purchased in Asian markets; if not available, use ⅓ lb. (150g) of regular dried noodles, which will yield 1 lb. (450g) noodles when cooked. Follow package directions for cooking.

■ This is a traditional Malaysian style pan-fried spicy noodle dish. Various kinds of meat may be used to substitute for chicken.

1

1 油3大匙燒熱，放入①料，炒
   至肉熟變白，蝦仁變紅，鏟
   於鍋邊。倒入②料略炒香，
   放入包心菜及熟麵，將所有
   鍋內材料炒拌均勻後，加入
   豆芽翻炒數下。

2 將麵盛於盤上，撒上③料即
   成。

* 熟油麵：可買現成的，或用
   一般乾麵4兩(150公克)煮
   熟，取代油麵12兩(450公
   克)。

■ 這道傳統的馬來式炒麵香辣
   可口。可用其他肉類取代雞
   肉。

檳城喇沙

< 2 人份 >

鯖魚（圖1）	12兩（450公克）

2	鹽	1½ 小匙
	糖	1小匙

3	鳳梨丁	¼ 杯
	紅蔥頭（切片）	2個
	紅辣椒（切絲）	2支
	黃瓜（去皮切絲）	½ 條

1	海鮮高湯	5杯
	基本辣醬泥（見19頁）	3大匙
	酸子汁	5大匙
	香茅（拍扁）	2支

辣草葉	20片

瀨粉*（圖2）	12兩（450公克）

Penang Noodle Soup *(Penang Asam Laksa)*

< SERVES 2 >

1 lb. (450g) mackerel (Fig.1)

1
- 5 c. seafood stock
- 3 T. basic chili paste (p.19)
- 5 T. tamarind juice
- 2 lemon grass, crushed

2
- 1½ t. salt
- 1 t. sugar

20 knotgrass leaves

3
- ¼ c. diced pineapple
- 2 shallots, sliced
- 2 shredded red chili peppers
- ½ cucumber, peeled and shredded

1 lb. (450g) Vietnamese rice noodles* (Fig.2)

1 Boil 1 in a pot. Add in fish and cook over medium heat for 6 minutes until fish is done. Take out the fish and remove bones. Retain the liquid.

2 Drain the retained liquid through a sieve then bring to boil. Add 2 and fish meat; bring to a boil again. Add knotgrass before turning off heat.

3 Blanch rice noodles and divide into two portions; place noodles in bowls. Divide 3 in half and put over the noodles, pour soup over the noodles.

* Rice noodles are similar to udon (Japanese noodles) but have a chewier texture. If not available, any kind of broad or thin dry rice sticks may be used as a substitute for the noodles.

■ Laksa is very popular in the city of Penang, Malaysia, as well as in Singapore and Indonesia. To get the special and unique flavor of this dish you must add knotgrass leaves. The sweet and sour flavor of the pineapple, when combined with the cucumber adds to the exotic taste of this soup.

1

2

1 將1料燒開,放入魚以中火煮6分鐘至魚熟,並撈出去骨取魚肉備用。

2 將煮魚湯過濾後燒開,加入2料及魚肉再煮開,最後加入辣草葉即可熄火。

3 將瀨粉川燙分盛於2大碗內,3料分別擺在麵上,淋上滾熱的魚肉湯即成。

* 瀨粉類似烏龍麵但比較Q,若無法購得也可用任何粗的或細乾米粉煮熟取代。

■ 檳城喇沙是馬來西亞檳城遠近馳名的小吃,在印尼、星加坡也很受歡迎。辣草葉是做喇沙不可缺少的香料,使湯麵別具特殊風味;鳳梨的酸甜加上黃瓜的口感,更顯出此湯麵的特色。

椰汁香飯

< 4 人份 >

米	2杯
蛋（打散）	1個
① 水 2杯，鹽 ½ 小匙	
法國香葉、香蘭葉	各3片
濃椰奶	4大匙
② 黃瓜（切片）	½ 條
辣椒絲，油蔥酥	各1大匙

1 鍋面塗少許油，將蛋煎成蛋皮，取出切絲備用。

2 米洗淨瀝乾，與①料混合，以電鍋煮熟，隨即倒入濃椰奶，攪拌均勻。

3 將飯盛於盤上，上置蛋皮絲及②料。食用時可配"辣炒小魚干"（見49頁）及"香炒椰絲牛肉片"（見80頁）。

■ 馬來西亞及印尼人通常將椰汁香飯當主食，尤其是當早餐。

Coconut Rice *(Nasi Lemak)*

< SERVES 4 >

2 c. rice	
1 egg, lightly beaten	
① 2 c. water, ½ t. salt	
3 ea.: bay leaves, pandan leaves	
4 T. thick coconut milk	
② ½ cucumber, sliced	
1 T. ea.: shredded chili pepper, crispy shallots (p.15)	

1 Coat a pan with a little oil. Pour in egg and rotate the pan to create a thin egg sheet. Remove and shred.

2 Wash and drain rice; mix with ①. Put in electric rice cooker* and cook. When cooked, add in coconut milk and mix well.

3 Remove rice to a serving plate; put ② and shredded egg sheet on top. Serve with "Spicy Anchovies" (p.49) and "Fried Grated Coconut with Beef" (p.81).

* If rice cooker is not available, bring rice and ① to boil over medium heat; reduce heat to low, cover and simmer for 20 minutes. Turn off heat and let stand for 10 minutes.

■ This dish is a main breakfast dish favorite with Malaysian and Indonesian people.

辣炒小魚干

< 2 人份 >

小魚乾*（圖1）	1杯
花生仁	4兩（150公克）
① 基本辣醬泥（見19頁）	3大匙
香茅（拍扁）	1支
② 鹽	⅛ 小匙（口味淡者免）
糖、酸子汁	各1大匙

1 小魚乾略洗淨以去鹹味，瀝乾。

2 炸油2杯燒熱，分別將小魚干及花生仁中火各炸至4分鐘至金黃色，撈出置於盤內待涼。

3 油3大匙燒熱，以小火炒香①料，再加入②料，略炒熄火後，將小魚干及花生仁一齊回鍋，炒拌均勻即可。

* 小魚乾是以鹽醃過曬乾的，可保存數個月不變質，選用的魚種類大小不限。此為著名小菜，與白飯或椰汁香飯（見49頁）配食，百吃不厭。

Spicy Anchovies *(Sambal Goreng Ikan Bilis)*

< SERVES 2 >

1 c. dried anchovies* (Fig.1)	
⅓ lb. (150g) unsalted peanuts	
① 3 T. basic chili paste (p.19)	
1 lemon grass, crushed	
② ⅛ t. salt, optional	
1 T. ea.: sugar, tamarind juice	

1 Briefly rinse anchovies to remove the salt; drain.

2 Heat 2 c. oil. Separately, deep-fry anchovies and then peanuts for 4 minutes each, until golden brown. Remove and drain, place on a plate and let cool.

3 Heat 3 T. oil; stir-fry ① over low heat until fragrant; add ② and briefly stir. Turn off heat, add anchovies and peanuts. Mix well, serve when cool.

* Anchovies are dried fish prepared in salt and are preserved in this manner indefinitely. This is a very famous side dish; often served with rice or "Coconut Rice" (p.49).

咖哩牛肉

< 4 人份 >

紅燒用牛瘦腿肉		12兩（450公克）
①	綜合辣醬泥（見19頁）	5大匙
	芫荽子粉、胡椒	各1大匙
	香茅 1支，丁香 6粒	
	肉桂（2.5公分）	1支
	小豆蔻 4粒，法國香葉 3片	
	小茴香子	1小匙
	椰奶	3杯
②	鹽、糖	各1小匙

1　牛肉切塊，以滾水川燙瀝乾。

2　油4大匙燒熱，炒香①料，加入牛肉拌炒均勻，再倒入椰奶燒開後，加入②料，改小火蓋鍋燜煮1½小時即成。

咖哩羊肉

用羊肉代替牛肉，其他材料及作法同上。

Beef Curry *(Kari Sapi)*

< SERVES 4 >

1 lb. (450g) beef (top round or London broil)	
① 5 T. mixed chili paste (p.19)	
1 T. ea.: coriander powder, pepper	
1 lemon grass , 6 cloves	
1 cinnamon stick, 1" (2.5cm)	
4 cardamom, 3 bay leaves	
1 t. cumin	
3 c. coconut milk	
② 1 t. ea.: salt, sugar	

1　Cut beef in pieces; blanch in boiling water. Remove and drain.

2　Heat 4T. oil; stir-fry ① until fragrant; add beef and mix well. Add coconut milk; bring to boil and add ②. Reduce heat to low, cover and cook 1½ hours.

Lamb Curry
Use lamb instead of beef. Other ingredients and cooking procedures are the same as above.

網狀餅

< 4 人份 >

	麵粉	1杯
①	雞蛋	2個
	鹽	¼ 小匙
	椰奶或牛奶	1杯
	牛油	適量

1　將①料攪拌均勻，徐徐倒入麵粉內，並加1大匙油攪成糊狀，裝入塑膠瓶內（圖1）。

2　牛油薄薄地抹上不沾鍋，將麵糊擠出條交叉來回成網狀，以小火每面煎約半分鐘至淡黃色，取出對折二次成三角形。配辛辣咖哩類的菜餚食用。

■　網狀餅及咖哩均是印度飲食文化流傳下來的菜餚，網狀餅通常是搭配牛肉咖哩或羊肉咖哩食用。

Lacy Pancakes *(Roti Jala)*

< SERVES 4 >

1 c. flour	
① 2 eggs	
¼ t. salt	
1 c. coconut milk or milk	
butter as desired	

1　Mix ① well; slowly, pour in flour and 1 T. oil; stir into a smooth batter. Pour into a plastic "squeeze" bottle (Fig.1).

2　Lightly coat the pan with a little butter. Squeeze batter into pan in a crisscross manner. Using low heat, pan-fry each side for 30 seconds until golden. Remove and fold twice toward the center to form a triangle. Best eaten with spicy dishes, such as curry.

■　Lacy pancakes are usually enjoyed with beef or lamb curry. Lacy pancakes and lamb curry originated in India.

1

椰汁蔬菜

< 4 人份 >

1	四季豆	8兩（300公克）
	合掌瓜（圖1）	4兩（150公克）
	胡蘿蔔	4兩（150公克）
2	玉米筍（切段）	4兩（150公克）
	辣椒（切條）	2支
3	蔥蒜醬泥（見19頁）	2大匙
	蝦米泥	2小匙
	黃薑粉	¼ 小匙
	法國香葉、南薑	各2片
	高湯	4杯
	鹽、糖	各1小匙
	椰奶	1杯

1 四季豆切段、合掌瓜削去外皮去核心後切塊，胡蘿蔔切塊備用。

2 將③料以大火燒開，加入①料再燒開，改中火煮至喜歡的熟軟度，加入②料，再加椰奶燒開即成。

■ 此菜餚有許多湯汁，但不屬於湯類；可淋在米飯上或配飯糰食用。

椰絲拌蔬菜

< 4 人份 >

	長豆（切段）	4兩（150公克）
1	菠菜（切段）	4兩（150公克）
	包心菜（切絲）	4兩（150公克）
	綠豆芽	4兩（150公克）
2	椰茸	1杯
	辣椒泥	2大匙
	蒜泥、芫荽子粉	各1小匙
	蝦醬、糖	各1小匙
	鹽	½ 小匙

1 將②料置碗內拌勻，以大火蒸15分鐘，或微波爐加熱3分鐘。

2 多量水燒開，將長豆煮5分鐘至軟，撈出沖冷水瀝乾；再分別將①料川燙，沖冷水瀝乾。全部加入蒸好的②料拌合。

■ 此道菜以數種蔬菜與椰茸等材料拌合而成，食用方法和沙拉相同。

Mixed Vegetables in Coconut Milk *(Sayur Lodeh)*

⎡ ⅔ lb. (300g) string beans
1 ⎸ ⅓ lb. (150g) chayote (Fig.1)
⎣ ⅓ lb. (150g) carrots

⎡ ⅓ lb. (150g) baby corn, cut
2 ⎸   into pieces
⎣ 2 chili peppers, cut in strips

⎡ 2 T. fragrant paste (p.19)
⎸ 2 t. ground dried shrimp
⎸ ¼ t. turmeric powder
3 ⎸ 2 bay leaves
⎸ 2 galangal slices
⎸ 4 c. stock
⎣ 1 t. ea.: salt, sugar

1 c. coconut milk

1 Cut string beans into sections. Peel skin and remove center of chayote, then cut to bite size pieces. Cut carrots into bite size pieces. Set aside.

2 Bring ③ to boil over high heat. Add ①, bring to boil again; reduce heat to medium, cook until desired tenderness is reached. Add ② and coconut milk. Bring to boil again. Serve.

■ This dish is made with many sauces, but is not classified as a soup. It is usually poured over rice or served with compressed rice balls.

1

Mixed Vegetables with Grated Coconut *(Urap Sayuran)*

⅓ lb. (150g) long beans,
    sectioned

⎡ ⅓ lb. (150g) ea.:
⎸   sectioned spinach,
1 ⎸   shredded cabbage,
⎣   bean sprouts

⎡ 1 c. shredded coconut
⎸ 2 T. ground fresh chilies
⎸ 1 t. ground fresh garlic
2 ⎸ 1 t. coriander powder
⎸ 1 t. shrimp paste (p.11)
⎸ 1 t. sugar
⎣ ½ t. salt

1 Mix ②, and steam 15 minutes over high heat or microwave at high for 3 minutes.

2 Boil a pot of water. Cook long beans 5 minutes until tender. Remove and rinse in cold water then drain. Blanch ingredients in ① separately, rinse in cold water and drain. Mix all vegetables with steamed ②. Serve.

■ This Malaysian dish is enjoyed as a "salad" when all the ingredients are combined and served with other dishes.

牛肉沙爹

< 4 人份 >

牛排肉	12兩（450公克）
蔥蒜醬泥（見19頁）	3大匙
黃薑粉	½ 小匙
芫荽子粉	2大匙
甜醬油	3大匙
糖	1小匙
鹽	¼ 小匙
香茅（拍扁）	1支
竹籤	20至25支

1 將牛肉切片，與①料拌勻，置於冰箱過夜。

2 將醃好的牛肉與4大匙油拌勻，取2-3片肉以竹籤串成肉串。預熱烤架（圖1）200℃（400℉），每面烤6分鐘。若用炭火烤風味更佳。

■ 上桌時可用黃瓜、紅蔥頭、鳳梨及飯糰等配食；與 "花生辣醬"（見19頁）沾食。此為南洋有名的菜餚，是大小宴會中必備的前菜，也可用來當主菜或零食。

雞肉沙爹 · 豬肉沙爹
用雞肉或豬肉代替牛肉，其他材料及作法同上。

Beef Sate *(Sate Daging)*

< SERVES 4 >

1 lb. (450g) beef (top sirloin)

☐
- **3 T. fragrant paste (p.19)**
- **½ t. turmeric powder**
- **2 T. coriander powder**
- **3 T. sweet soy sauce**
- **1 t. sugar**
- **¼ t. salt**
- **1 lemon grass, crushed**

20 to 25 skewers

1 Slice beef and marinate in ☐ in refrigerator overnight.

2 Mix beef with 4 T. oil and place 2 or 3 slices on a skewer at a time. Pre-heat electric grill (Fig.1) to 400°F (200°C), and grill each side 6 minutes (may use charcoal barbeque for enhanced flavor).

■ Best served and enjoyed with cucumbers, shallots, pineapple and compressed rice; dip in "Peanut Sambal" (p.19). This is by far, the most popular and favorite grilled dish in Indonesia, Malaysia and Singapore. May be served as a snack, appetizer or main dish.

Pork Sate · Chicken Sate
Substitute pork or chicken for beef. Other ingredients and cooking procedures are the same as above.

Compressed Rice *(Lontong)*

< SERVES 4 >

2 c. rice

☐
- **3 c. water**
- **¼ t. salt**
- **3 pandan leaves**

4 pieces of aluminum foil, 10 ¾" x 12" (27 cm x 30cm)

2

1 Wash and rinse rice; add ☐. Place in electric rice cooker* (when done, rice should be more moist than usual). While hot, mash the rice then divide into 4 portions.

2 Place one portion of rice on each aluminum sheet, roll up and twist the ends closed. The tighter the better. Set aside to cool (Fig.2).

3 Remove rice from foil, cut into slices. Serve with "Mixed Vegetables with Grated Coconut" (p.53), and any desired spicy meat.

* If rice cooker is not available, soak rice in water overnight then drain. Bring rice and ☐ to boil over medium heat; reduce heat to low, cover, and simmer for 20 minutes. Turn off heat and let stand for 10 minutes.

■ Banana leaves are the authentic and traditional method of wrapping and compressing the rice. However, for convenience purposes aluminum foil will produce similar results.

飯糰

< 4 人 份 >

米	2杯
水	3杯
鹽	¼ 小匙
香蘭葉	3片
鋁箔紙（27公分x30公分）	4張

☐

1 米洗淨瀝乾加入①料，放入電鍋內煮熟，煮成的飯軟度會超過一般的米飯，乘熱以飯匙稍壓扁使不成粒狀，分成四份。

2 分別將飯置於鋁箔紙中間，捲緊成長筒狀，兩端用力捏緊成糖果狀（越緊越好），放一邊待涼（圖2）。

3 打開鋁紙切片食用。可與 "椰汁蔬菜"（見52頁）及辛辣肉類配食。

■ 傳統作法是以香蕉葉包裹飯糰，若就地取材使用鋁箔紙來包裹，不僅方便效果也不錯。

茄汁辣牛尾

< 4 人份 >

	牛尾(圖1)	1斤(600公克)
1	基本辣醬泥(見19頁)	3大匙
	番茄醬	3大匙
	酸子汁	1½ 大匙
	黃薑粉	¼ 小匙
	香茅(拍扁)	1支
	南薑	2片
	檸檬葉	6片
2	鹽、胡椒	各1小匙
	糖	1大匙

1 牛尾切塊,以滾水川燙,將①料與牛尾拌勻,醃過夜。

2 將醃好的牛尾加4杯水燒開,加入②料改中火,蓋鍋燜煮1½小時至牛尾熟爛,餘汁成稀糊狀。

■ 此道菜內加番茄醬,主要是受到歐洲飲食文化的影響,並綜合南洋口味,因而菜餚味香濃,可用來淋飯或淋麵,是為一般的家庭菜。

香料牛肉湯

< 4 人份 >

	紅燒用牛瘦腿肉12兩(450公克)	
1	薑 1小塊,肉桂(2.5公分) 1支	
	法國香葉 3片,豆蔻 ½ 粒	
	丁香、小豆蔻	各6粒
	蒜頭	6個
2	胡椒	½ 小匙
	鹽 1½ 小匙,糖 1小匙	
3	油蔥酥、芹菜葉(切絲)各2大匙	
	芫荽葉	2大匙
	番茄(切塊)	2個

1 牛肉切塊,以滾水川燙。

2 水10杯、①料及牛肉燒開,改小火蓋鍋煮1½小時至牛肉湯汁剩6杯,加入②料即為牛肉湯。

3 將牛肉湯盛於碗內,加入③料即成。

■ 香料牛肉湯味香濃,可拌飯或粉絲食用。

香料羊肉湯 · 香料牛尾湯

用羊肉或牛尾代替牛肉,其他材料及作法同上。

Oxtail in Hot Tomato Sauce *(Buntut Saus Tomat)*

< SERVES 4 >

1⅓ lbs. (600g) oxtail (Fig.1)

1
- **3 T. basic chili paste (p.19)**
- **3 T. ketchup**
- **1½ T. tamarind juice**
- **¼ t. turmeric powder**
- **1 lemon grass, crushed**
- **2 galangal slices**
- **6 kaffir leaves**

2
- **1 t. ea.: salt, pepper**
- **1 T. sugar**

1. Cut oxtail into pieces, blanch in boiling water. Marinate in ① overnight.

2. Boil marinated oxtails in 4 c. water. Add ②, reduce heat to medium; cover and cook 1½ hours until oxtails are tender and the sauce thickens slightly.

■ The use of ketchup in this dish is influenced by strong European cultural tastes, and when combined with the Southeast Asian flavors, produces a most delectable taste. Can pour on rice or noodles to make a very popular and typical family dish.

1

Aromatic Spiced Beef Soup *(Sop Sapi)*

< SERVES 4 >

1 lb. (450g) beef (top round or London broil)

1
- **1 piece ginger root**
- **1 cinnamon stick, 1" (2.5cm)**
- **3 bay leaves**
- **½ nutmeg**
- **6 ea.: cloves, cardamom**
- **6 garlic cloves**

2
- **½ t. pepper**
- **1½ t. salt**
- **1 t. sugar**

3
- **2 T. crispy shallots (p.15)**
- **2 T. shredded celery leaves**
- **2 T. cilantro**
- **2 tomatoes, cut in pieces**

1. Cut beef into bite size pieces and blanch in boiling water.

2. Place ① and beef in 10 c. water; bring to boil. Reduce heat to low, cover and cook 1½ hours until the liquid is reduced to 6 cups. Add ② to complete the beef soup.

3. Pour beef soup in a bowl, add ③ and serve.

■ This soup has a very fragrant aroma and is delicious when served with rice or glass noodles.

Aromatic Spiced Lamb Soup · Aromatic Spiced Oxtail Soup
Use lamb or oxtail instead of beef. Other ingredients and cooking procedures are the same as above.

香料燜雞

< 2 人 份 >

雞腿(切塊)		1斤(600公克)
粉絲(圖1)		半兩(20公克)
馬鈴薯(切塊)		1個
1	紅蔥頭泥、蒜泥	各1大匙
	洋蔥(切片)	½ 個
	豆蔻(略壓) ½ 粒，丁香 5粒	
	番茄塊	1杯
2	甜醬油 4大匙，鹽 1小匙	
	水	1杯
	油蔥酥	2大匙

1 粉絲泡軟，馬鈴薯切塊炸熟至表面呈金黃色。

2 油或牛油3大匙，將1料內的材料依序放入炒香，隨入雞塊炒至變色，加2料燒開，改小火蓋鍋燜煮25分鐘，加入炸好的馬鈴薯，最後加入粉絲略翻拌，盛起撒上油蔥酥。

Aromatic Stewed Chicken *(Semur Ayam)*

< SERVES 2 >

1⅓ lbs. (600g) chicken legs,
    cut in pieces
⅔ oz. (20g) packaged glass
    noodles (Fig.1)
1 potato, cut in pieces

1.
- 1 T. ground shallots
- 1 T. ground fresh garlic
- ½ onion, sliced
- ½ nutmeg, slightly crushed
- 5 cloves, 1 c. tomato pieces

2.
- 4 T. sweet soy sauce
- 1 t. salt, 1 c. water

2 T. crispy shallots (p.15)

1. Soak glass noodles in water to soften. Deep-fry potatoes until golden brown; remove.

2. Stir-fry ① in 3 T. oil or butter until fragrant. Add chicken; stir-fry until color changes; add ② bring to boil, turn to low heat, cover and cook 25 minutes. Add potatoes, then glass noodles and mix well. Serve with crispy shallots (p.15) sprinkled on top.

Spicy and Sour Chicken *(Ayam Sambal Asam)*

< SERVES 2 >

1⅓ lbs. (600g) chicken legs

1.
- 1 t. ea.: salt, lime juice

oil for deep-frying

2.
- 5 T. basic chili paste (p.19)
- 1 t. ground ginger root
- 1 lemon grass, sliced

3.
- 3 T. tamarind juice
- ½ t. salt
- 1 T. ea.: sugar, water

1. Cut chicken into pieces; Rub with ①; let stand for 1 hour. Pat dry; deep-fry over medium heat for 8 minutes until golden brown.

2. Stir-fry ② in 4 T. oil until fragrant; add ③ and let boil. Add in cooked chicken and mix well. Sprinkle on shredded kaffir leaves, if desired.

■ This is a favorite family dish when combined with rice, because pan-frying the chicken in this way makes it crispy and aromatic. In step 2, 4 T. oil is used for stir-frying, since this amount is essential to get the desired result.

酸辣燒雞

< 2 人份 >

雞腿	1斤(600公克)

1.
鹽、青檸檬汁	各1小匙
炸油	適量

2.
基本辣醬泥(見19頁)	5大匙
薑泥	1小匙
香茅(切片)	1支

3.
酸子汁	3大匙
鹽	½小匙
糖、水	各1大匙

1. 雞腿切塊，以①料醃1小時拭乾，放入油內中火炸8分鐘至熟呈金黃色。

2. 油4大匙炒香②料，加入③料燒開，將炸雞加入拌炒即成。可撒上少許檸檬葉絲。

■ 炒出來的雞塊乾香，是很下飯的家庭菜。唯作法②內的炒菜油量，需比一般炒菜用油量要多一些。

蝦醬炸魚

<　　4 人份　　>

魚排	12兩（450公克）
1 鹽	½ 小匙
青檸檬汁	1大匙
2 基本辣醬泥（見19頁）	5大匙
蝦米泥	1大匙
蝦醬	1小匙
香茅（拍扁）	1支
糖	1大匙
炸油	適量

1　魚排洗淨，拭乾以①料醃30分鐘後再拭乾水份。

2　炸油燒熱，將魚排放入油內，大火炸6分鐘至魚肉剛熟，表面呈金黃色撈出。

3　油4大匙燒熱，炒香②料，加入糖略炒，即可淋在炸好的魚排上，可用香茅葉撕成絲當裝飾。

■　此為利用東南亞一帶出產的蝦醬所做出來的菜餚，口味獨特，非常下飯，冷或熱食皆可，一次做多些可分次取食。

娘惹酸甜魚

<　　2 人份　　>

魚（1條）	1斤（600公克）
1 鹽、青檸檬汁	各1小匙
2 洋蔥（切片）	½ 個
蒜頭（拍碎）	2個
薑	4片
3 番茄塊	1杯
辣椒絲	2大匙
4 水 1杯，鹽 ½ 小匙	
糖、醋、番茄醬　各1½ 大匙	
5 太白粉 1小匙，水 1大匙	

1　在魚肉厚處劃刀痕（圖1），以①料醃30分鐘後拭乾水份，沾少許太白粉。

2　油4大匙燒熱，中火將魚兩面各煎2分鐘至表面呈金黃色鏟於一邊，餘油炒香②料，隨入③料略炒，將魚鏟至鍋中加④料煮5分鐘至魚肉熟，鏟出盛於盤上，餘汁以⑤料勾芡後加入1大匙油，淋在魚上，非常下飯。

■　此道菜承襲自先母的祖傳秘方，特別有味道。

1

Fried Fish in Shrimp Paste Chili Sauce *(Ikan Sambal Belacan)*

< SERVES 4 >

1 lb. (450g) fish fillet

☐1
½ t. salt
1 T. lime juice

☐2
5 T. basic chili paste (p.19)
1 T. ground dried shrimp
1 t. shrimp paste (p.11)
1 lemon grass, crushed

1 T. sugar
oil for deep-frying

1 Wash fish and pat dry. Rub with ☐1; let stand for 30 minutes, pat dry again.

2 Heat oil; deep-fry fish over high heat for 6 minutes, until just cooked and golden brown. Remove.

3 Heat 4 T. oil; stir-fry ☐2 until aromatic. Add sugar, lightly stir and pour on fish. May garnish with lemon grass leaves.

■ Shrimp paste is a favorite with the people of Southeast Asia; this dish, in particular, uses this flavoring to derive its unique and special taste. It goes well with rice and can be enjoyed hot or cold. For convenience, a large amount can be prepared at one time, and portions served over time as desired.

Nyonya Sweet and Sour Fish *(Ikan Asam Manis Nyonya)*

< SERVES 2 >

1⅓ lb. (600g) fish

☐1 1 t. ea.: salt, lime juice

☐2
½ onion, sliced
2 garlic cloves, crushed
4 ginger root slices

☐3
1 c. tomato pieces
2 T. shredded chili peppers

☐4
1 c. water
½ t. salt
1½ T. ea.: sugar, vinegar
1½ T. ketchup

☐5
1 t. cornstarch
1 T. water

1 Score fish in thick areas (Fig.1); Rub with ☐1; let stand for 30 minutes, pat dry. Lightly coat fish with cornstarch.

2 Heat 4 T. oil; pan-fry fish over medium heat for 2 minutes, until both sides are golden brown; move to side of pan. Stir-fry ☐2 in remaining oil, until aromatic, add ☐3 and lightly stir-fry. Move fish back to center; add ☐4 and cook 5 minutes, until fish is cooked. Remove fish and put on a plate. Add ☐5 to the remaining mixture in the pan; stir to thicken and add 1 T. oil. Pour over fish; serve with rice.

■ This is a very special and tasty dish created by my mother that is often served and enjoyed by our family and friends.

香汁魚

<　4 人 份　>

	魚排	12兩（450公克）
①	鹽	½ 小匙
	青檸檬汁	1小匙
②	臘仁辣醬泥（見19頁）	4大匙
	黃薑粉	½ 小匙
	南薑（拍扁）	2片
	香茅（拍扁）	1支
	檸檬葉	6片
	椰奶	2杯
③	鹽、糖	各1小匙
	酸子汁	2大匙
	辣椒（直切半）	3支

1　魚排洗淨拭乾，以①料醃30分鐘備用。

2　將②料攪勻以中火燒開，改小火煮5分鐘至香味溢出，加入③料及魚排，以中火再煮5分鐘至魚肉熟，最後加入辣椒即可。

■　此為印尼及星馬一帶，大小餐廳都可見到的普遍菜餚，非常開胃，冷熱食皆可。

黃汁鮮魷

<　4 人 份　>

	魷魚*	12兩（450公克）
①	鹽 ½ 小匙，青檸檬汁 1大匙	
②	蔥蒜醬泥（見19頁）	3大匙
	黃薑粉、鹽	各½ 小匙
	南薑（略拍）	2片
	香茅（拍扁）	1支
	法國香葉	3片
	椰奶	1杯
③	胡椒、糖	各1小匙

1　魷魚以①料略醃。

2　將②料攪勻以中火燒開，改小火煮5分鐘至香味溢出，加入魷魚及③料，大火燒開再煮5分鐘至魷魚熟，汁濃稠即可。隨意撒上油蔥酥及芫荽葉，冷熱食均可。

*　印馬沿海盛產新鮮魷魚，燒出來的濃汁鮮美可口，若無可用冷凍魷魚取代（圖1）。

Fish in Spicy Coconut Gravy *(Gulai Ikan)*

1 lb. (450g) fish fillet

☐1
- **½ t. salt**
- **1 t. lime juice**

☐2
- **4 T. candlenut chili paste (p.19)**
- **½ t. turmeric powder**
- **2 galangal slices, crushed**
- **1 lemon grass, crushed**
- **6 kaffir leaves**
- **2 c. coconut milk**

☐3
- **1 t. ea.: salt, sugar**
- **2 T. tamarind juice**

3 chili peppers, cut in half lengthwise

1 Wash fish and pat dry. Rub with ☐1; let stand for 30 minutes.

2 Mix ☐2 over medium heat; bring to boil. Reduce heat to low and cook for 5 minutes. Add ☐3 and the fish; cook 5 more minutes over medium heat. Add chili peppers and serve.

■ This is a very popular dish served in restaurants in Malaysia, Indonesia and Singapore. This dish can be eaten hot or cold as an appetite enhancer.

1

Squid in Yellow Sauce *(Sotong Masak Kuning)*

1 lb. (450g) squid*

☐1
- **½ t. salt**
- **1 T. lime juice**

☐2
- **3 T. fragrant paste (p.19)**
- **½ t. ea.: turmeric powder, salt**
- **2 galangal slices, slightly crushed**
- **1 lemon grass, crushed**
- **3 bay leaves**
- **1 c. coconut milk**

☐3
- **1 t. ea.: pepper, sugar**

1 Rub squid with ☐1 and remove excess.

2 Mix ☐2 over medium heat; bring to boil. Turn to low and cook 5 minutes. Add in squid and ☐3; cook 5 minutes over high heat until squid curls and sauce thickens slightly. If desired, sprinkle on crispy shallots (p.15) and cilantro. May be served either hot or cold.

* Along the coasts of Indonesia and Malaysia, squid is abundant. The use of fresh squid guarantees the truest flavor; however, frozen squid (Fig.1) may be substituted for fresh squid.

辣醬炒蝦仁

< 2 人 份 >

	蝦仁	6兩（225公克）
☐1	臘仁辣醬泥（見19頁）	4大匙
	番茄（切丁）	1杯
	香茅（拍扁）	1支
☐2	鹽	½ 小匙
	糖	1小匙
	青檸檬汁	1大匙
	水	¼ 杯

1 油3大匙燒熱，炒香☐1料，待番茄炒軟後，加☐2料燒開，再加入蝦仁拌炒至變色熟了，汁呈濃稠狀即可。

■ 這道菜簡單易做又下飯，是先母的居家常備菜。

Shrimp in Red Hot Sauce
(Sambal Goreng Udang)

< SERVES 2 >

	½ lb. (225g) shelled shrimp
☐1	4 T. candlenut chili paste (p.19)
	1 c. tomato, diced
	1 lemon grass, crushed
☐2	½ t. salt
	1 t. sugar
	1 T. lime juice
	¼ c. water

1 Heat 3 T. oil; stir-fry ☐1 until aromatic. When tomato softens, add ☐2 and bring to boil. Stir in shrimp, cook until shrimp changes color and sauce thickens. Serve.

■ This dish is very easy to make and goes well with rice.

玉米蝦餅

< 2 人 份 >

	蝦仁	6兩（225公克）
	玉米粒	1½ 杯
☐1	鹽	½ 小匙
	糖、胡椒	各1小匙
	芫荽子粉、辣椒粉	各½ 大匙
	雞蛋	1個
	麵粉	3大匙
	炸油	適量

1 將蝦仁、玉米粒與☐1料一起倒入攪拌器攪細，再加入蛋及麵粉，攪拌成蝦絨。

2 炸油適量燒熱，舀一大湯匙蝦絨，放入鍋中，以中火炸4分鐘至金黃色。一共可以做14個，趁熱沾"花生辣醬"（見17頁）與"椰汁香飯"（見49頁）食用。

■ 蝦餅略似炸蝦球，因內加玉米粒及芫荽子粉，外皮鬆脆內香嫩，很適合老人或小孩食用，除當主菜外也可當前菜或點心，玉米粒可選擇新鮮、冷凍或罐裝。

Corn and Shrimp Fritters
(Perkedel Jagung)

< SERVES 2 >

	½ lb. (225g) shelled shrimp
	1½ c. corn kernels
☐1	½ t. salt
	1 t. ea.: sugar, pepper
	½ T. ea.: coriander powder, chili powder
	1 egg
	3 T. flour
	oil for deep-frying

1 Combine shrimp, corn and ☐1 in a blender and grind. Add egg, flour, and mix to form shrimp mixture.

2 Heat oil; spoon out shrimp mixture into a pan. Deep-fry 4 minutes until golden brown. Makes 14 fritters. Serve while hot with "Peanut Sambal" (p.17) as a dip. Goes well with "Coconut Rice" (p.49). Also makes a great appetizer or snack.

■ Shrimp fritters are similar to fried shrimp balls. The addition of corn kernels and coriander powder makes the outside very crispy, while maintaining a soft inside. Popular with older people and young children and can be made with either fresh, frozen or canned corn kernels. Can be served as a main dish, appetizer or snack.

椰子糖西米布丁

<　8 個　>

	西米*（圖1）	6兩（225公克）
①	水	8杯
	鹽	¼ 小匙
②	椰子糖（壓碎）	1杯
	糖	1大匙
	水	⅓ 杯
③	濃椰奶	¾ 杯
	鹽	¼ 小匙

1　將①料燒開，加入西米，改小火煮5分鐘，熄火蓋鍋燜10分鐘撈出，以冷水略沖洗去黏液後瀝乾，分盛於八個小碗，放入冰箱備用。

2　將②料以小火煮開成椰子糖漿；③料用微波爐加熱40秒。

3　食用時將冰冷的西米倒扣在盤上，淋上椰子糖漿及濃椰奶。

*　西米是從棕櫚樹果實中提煉出來的澱粉，製成硬粒狀，水煮後呈透明狀。

■　這是一道可口老少咸宜的飯後甜點，在馬來西亞的大街小巷均可買到。

椰子糖糯米糕

<　1 2 塊　>

	糯米	2杯
	香蘭葉	3片
①	濃椰奶	5大匙
	椰子糖（壓碎）	6兩（225公克）

1　糯米洗淨，浸泡隔夜。瀝乾後放入1½杯水及香蘭葉煮成糯米飯。

2　將①料以小火燒開，糖溶化後與熱的糯米飯翻拌，再倒入模型（20公分x20公分）內壓緊（圖2），待冷切塊。

■　糯米糕若久置冰箱會變硬，可先用微波爐加熱變軟後，再置冰箱略冰涼切塊食用。

Coconut Tapioca Pudding *(Sago Malaka)*

< 8 SERVINGS >

½ lb. (225g) tapioca pearls* (Fig.1)

① 8 c. water
¼ t. salt

② 1 c. palm sugar, crushed
1 T. sugar
⅓ c. water

③ ¾ c. thick coconut milk
¼ t. salt

1 Bring ① to boil; add tapioca, reduce heat to low and cook 5 minutes. Turn off heat, cover and let set 10 minutes. Remove and rinse in cold water, drain. Divide into 8 bowls and place in refrigerator.

2 Bring ② to boil over low heat to make syrup. Place ③ in microwave for 40 seconds.

3 Remove bowls from refrigerator. Invert each bowl onto a plate; remove the bowl and pour the syrup and mixture ③ over the tapioca.

* A hard kernel form of starch from a palm tree, which becomes transparent after cooking, available in markets.

■ This is a very popular dessert for all ages and can be found throughout Malaysia.

1

2

Sticky Rice Cake *(Wajik)*

< MAKES 12 >

2 c. glutinous rice
3 pandan leaves

① 5 T. thick coconut milk
½ lb. (225g) palm sugar,
    crushed

1 Wash rice, soak in water overnight. Drain and add 1½ c. water and pandan leaves, cook in rice cooker*.

2 Bring ① to boil over low heat, cook until palm sugar melts and mix with hot rice. Pack tightly into an 8"x 8" (20cm x 20cm) container (Fig.2) and let cool. Cut and serve.

* If rice cooker is not available, place rice and pandan leaves in container and steam over medium heat for 30 minutes.

■ If refrigerated over a long time, the rice cake will become hard. Warming it in a microwave will soften; briefly cool the cake in the refrigerator before slicing.

黃薑糯米飯

Sticky Yellow Rice *(Nasi Kunjit)*

< 4 人份 >

< SERVES 4 >

長糯米	2杯
水 ¾ 杯，濃椰奶 ½ 杯	
① 鹽 1小匙，黃薑粉 ¼ 小匙	
香蘭葉	2片
青檸檬汁	1小匙

2 c. long glutinous rice	
¾ c. water, ½ c. thick coconut milk	
① 1 t. salt, ¼ t. turmeric powder	
2 big pandan leaves	
1 t. lime juice	

1 糯米洗淨浸泡過夜。

2 將米瀝乾與①料拌勻放入電鍋內煮熟成飯，加青檸檬汁拌勻即成。

■ 在蘇門答臘島 "黃薑糯米飯"，是任何喜慶宴會中必備之米飯，通常與 "乾辣醬燒雞"（見69頁）和 "辣味全蛋"（見73頁）等等的香辣菜餚一起食用。

1 Wash rice and soak in water overnight.

2 Drain rice; mix with ① and put in a rice cooker*. After rice is cooked, mix with lime juice.

* If a rice cooker is not available, steam the rice in a steamer over high heat for 15 minutes until semi-cooked. Omit ¾ c. water and bring the remaining ingredients in ① to boil; add in lime juice then mix well with semi-cooked rice and steam again over medium heat for 25 minutes until rice is cooked.

■ This is a popular and favorite dish at parties, banquets weddings, etc. on the island of Sumatra. Goes well with "Eggs in Spicy Red Sauce" (p.73), and "Spicy Chicken Braised in Coconut Milk" (p.69), or any other spicy meat.

乾辣醬燒雞

Spicy Chicken Braised in Coconut Milk *(Rendang Ayam)*

< 4 人份 >

< SERVES 4 >

雞	2斤4兩（1350公克）
① 鹽 1小匙，青檸檬汁 1大匙	
椰奶	2杯
② 綜合辣醬泥（見19頁）	12大匙
香茅（拍扁）	2支
檸檬葉	6片
濃椰奶	1杯
③ 酸子汁	1大匙
鹽、糖	各1小匙

3 lbs. (1350g) chicken	
① 1 t. salt, 1 T. lime juice	
2 c. coconut milk	
② 12 T. mixed chili paste (p.19)	
2 lemon grass, crushed	
6 kaffir leaves	
1 c. thick coconut milk	
③ 1 T. tamarind juice	
1 t. ea.: salt, sugar	

1 雞切半或切塊，以①料醃1小時。

2 將②料煮開，改中火煮5分鐘至汁稍濃，加入雞塊，以大火燒開後，改小火蓋鍋煮20分鐘，煮時需將雞塊翻面。

3 再加③料以中火再煮10分鐘至雞熟，汁變濃稠。

■ 雞汁的濃稠度依個人喜好決定，一些人喜歡煮久些讓汁收乾，出紅油為止。

1 Cut chicken in half or in pieces. Rub with ①; let stand for 1 hour.

2 Bring ② to boil; reduce heat to medium and cook 5 minutes until sauce has slightly thickened. Add chicken and bring to boil over high heat. Reduce heat to low, cover and cook 20 minutes, stirring occasionally.

3 Add ③; cook 10 more minutes over medium heat, until chicken is cooked and sauce has thickened. Serve.

■ Thickness of the chicken sauce may be determined by personal taste. If desired, you may continue the cooking until the sauce is evaporated and red chili oil appears.

香料鳳梨雞飯

< 4人份 >

	雞胸或雞腿肉	12兩（450公克）
	米	2杯
1	紅蔥頭泥、蒜泥	各½ 大匙
	薑泥	1小匙
	芫荽子粉、胡椒	各1小匙
2	豆蔻（略拍）	½ 粒
	丁香	4粒
	小茴香子	¼ 小匙
	小豆蔻	3粒
	香茅（拍扁）	1支
3	高湯	2½ 杯
	鹽	1小匙
	鳳梨丁	1杯
	油蔥酥	2大匙

1 雞切塊、米洗淨瀝乾備用。

2 油2大匙燒熱，小火炒香1料，加入2料續炒3分鐘至香味溢出，加入雞塊，以大火拌炒至雞肉變色，再倒入3料燒開，改中火續煮5分鐘至肉熟撈出，剩餘的雞湯2杯備用。

3 將雞湯與米倒入電鍋內煮，飯熟後立刻將炒好的雞塊加入攪拌均勻。

4 將飯盛於大盤上，鳳梨丁圍在四週，隨意撒上油蔥酥、香菜、辣椒等。

■ 受印度飲食文化的影響，此道菜使用多種印度香料來調味，再配上鳳梨丁更有酸甜味，增加此道菜的風味，是理想的簡餐。

Pineapple Chicken Rice
(Nasi Kebuli Ayam)

< SERVES 4 >

1 lb. (450g) boneless chicken breast or chicken legs	
2 c. rice	
1	½ T. ea.: ground shallots, ground fresh garlic
	1 t. ground ginger root
	1 t. ea.: coriander powder, pepper
2	½ nutmeg, slightly crushed
	4 cloves
	¼ t. cumin
	3 cardamom
	1 lemon grass, crushed
3	2½ c. stock
	1 t. salt
	1 c. diced pineapple
	2 T. crispy shallots (p.15)

1 Cut chicken into bite size pieces. Wash rice, drain and set aside.

2 Heat 2 T. oil; stir-fry 1 over low heat until aromatic. Add 2 and stir 3 minutes. Add chicken pieces; stir-fry over high heat until chicken changes color. Add 3; bring to boil, reduce heat to medium and cook 5 minutes or until chicken is cooked. Remove chicken and reserve 2 c. of the stock for cooking rice.

3 Place 2 c. of reserved stock and rice in rice cooker*. After rice is cooked, stir in chicken pieces immediately.

4 Place rice mixture in a plate, arrange pineapple around the plate and sprinkle on crispy shallots (p.15), cilantro, and chili peppers as desired.

* If rice cooker is not available, bring rice and 2 c. stock to boil over medium heat; reduce heat to low, cover and simmer for 20 minutes. Turn off heat and let stand for 10 minutes.

■ Because of the influence of the Indian culture, many traditional Indian spices are used in this dish. Ideal when eaten with diced pineapple, creating a wonderful sweet and sour taste.

香草椰汁飯

< 4 人份 >

米		2杯
①	水 2杯，鹽 ½ 小匙	
	香茅（拍扁）	1支
	南薑 3片，香蘭葉 2片	
	濃椰奶	4大匙
②	檸檬葉（切絲）	3片
	香茅（切薄片）	½ 支
	芫荽葉、黃瓜（去皮）	各10片
	辣草葉或九層塔	5片
	紅蔥頭（切薄片）	1個

1 米洗淨瀝乾與①料混合用電鍋煮熟。

2 將飯與②料拌均勻，喜食辣者可加辣椒絲，配上"辣味全蛋"（見72頁）或辛辣肉類均可。

■ 白色米飯拌各種顏色的香草葉，再配上金黃色的蛋及辛辣肉類，是一道色香味俱全的全餐。

Fragrant Coconut Rice *(Nasi Kerabu)*

< SERVES 4 >

2 c. rice	
① 2 c. water, ½ t. salt	
1 lemon grass, crushed	
3 galangal slices, 2 pandan leaves	
4 T. thick coconut milk	
② 3 kaffir leaves, shredded	
½ lemon grass, sliced	
10 ea.: cilantro leaves, peeled cucumber slices	
5 knotgrass or basil leaves	
1 shallot, thinly sliced	

1 Wash rice and drain; mix with ①; cook in rice cooker*.

2 Mix ② with cooked rice. Shredded chili pepper may be added as desired. Serve with "Eggs in Spicy Red Sauce" (p.72) or other spicy meat.

* If rice cooker is not available, bring rice and ① to boil over medium heat; reduce heat to low, cover and simmer for 20 minutes. Turn off heat and let stand for 10 minutes.

■ This is a very colorful and delicious meal because of the white rice, various colorful herbs, golden brown eggs and spicy meat.

辣味全蛋

< 6 個 >

水煮蛋（去殼）		6個
炸油		適量
①	基本辣醬泥（見19頁）	4大匙
	鹽	½小匙
	番茄丁	¾杯
	香茅（拍扁）	1支
②	青檸檬汁、糖	各1大匙
	水	2大匙

1 炸油燒熱，將蛋放入油內中火炸3分鐘至表面呈金黃色撈出。

2 油3大匙燒熱，炒香①料續入②料，略煮至汁濃稠，隨即加入炸好之全蛋，拌炒均勻即可。

■ 此為很受歡迎的食攤小菜，香辣可口，是非常美味的配飯菜，也很適合當前菜。

Eggs in Spicy Red Sauce *(Telor Balado)*

< MAKES 6 >

6 hard-boiled eggs (shelled)	
oil for deep-frying	
① 4 T. basic chili paste (p.19)	
½ t. salt	
¾ c. diced tomatoes	
1 lemon grass, crushed	
② 1 T. ea.: lime juice, sugar	
2 T. water	

1 Heat oil then deep-fry the eggs over medium heat for 3 minutes until golden brown; remove.

2 Heat 3 T. oil; stir-fry ① until aromatic, add in ② and slightly cook until sauce thickens. Add eggs and mix well. Serve.

■ This delicious spicy dish is very popular and served in restaurants and among street vendors. Eaten as a main dish with rice, or as an appetizer, and a favorite at potluck dinners.

爪哇沙拉

< 4 人 份 >

①	菠菜（切段）	8兩（300公克）
	包心菜（切片）	4兩（150公克）
②	四季豆（切段）	4兩（150公克）
	合掌瓜（圖1）（去皮切塊）	
		4兩（150公克）
	炸豆腐（切塊）	4兩（150公克）
	水煮蛋（直切半）	2個
	油蔥酥	2大匙
	花生辣醬（見17頁）	½ 杯

1　將多量水燒開，加入1小匙鹽及1大匙油，分別將①料川燙，撈出瀝乾備用。再將水燒開，放入②料煮開，改成中火煮約5分鐘，撈出瀝乾。

2　將燙熟的全部蔬菜及炸豆腐盛於大盤上，蛋放在菜上面，淋上花生辣醬，再撒上油蔥酥。

■　此菜在印尼的路邊攤或餐廳非常流行，也有婦女背著一籃煮好的青菜販賣，要買的時候再淋上花生辣醬，是一道可當正餐或點心的傳統家常菜餚。

椰汁蝦仁菠菜

< 4 人 份 >

	菠菜	8兩（300公克）
	合掌瓜（圖1）	½ 個
	蝦仁	4兩（150公克）
①	紅蔥頭（切片）	3粒
	香茅（拍扁）	1支
	辣椒泥	1大匙
	蝦醬	1小匙
②	高湯、椰奶	各1杯
③	鹽	½ 小匙
	糖	1小匙

1　將菠菜切段川燙，合掌瓜切塊煮5分鐘撈出。

2　將①加②料燒開，改小火煮5分鐘至出味，加入③料及蝦仁略煮，隨即倒入燙好的蔬菜，再燒開即成。

■　為保持蔬菜之青綠，煮蔬菜時在多量水內加少許鹽及油；此道菜可拌白飯或淋在"飯糰"（見55頁）上，配上辛辣的肉類即成均衡的正餐。

Java Salad with Peanut Sauce *(Gado-Gado)*

1 ⎡ ⅔ lb. (300g) spinach,
     cut in sections
   ⎣ ⅓ lb. (150g) cabbage, sliced

2 ⎡ ⅓ lb. (150g) cut string beans
     ⅓ lb. (150g) peeled chayote
   ⎣ (Fig.1), cut in pieces

⅓ lb. (150g) fried regular
   tofu, cut in pieces
2 hard-boiled eggs,
   cut in half lengthwise
2 T. crispy shallots (p.15)
½ c. peanut sambal (p.17)

1 Bring large amount of water to a boil. Add 1 t. salt and 1 T. oil. Separately, blanch ingredients in ①. Remove and set aside. Boil water again, add ② and bring to boil, reduce heat to medium; cook 5 minutes, remove and drain.

2 Place cooked vegetables and regular tofu in a plate, add eggs on top. Pour on peanut sambal and sprinkle on crispy shallots and then serve.

■ An Indonesian favorite, may be purchased from street vendors and from the restaurants. Traditionally, Indonesian women carry a basket with the cooked vegetables on their head and sell them on streets. When purchased, they pour the peanut sambal on them and serve. A family dish that is popular as a meal or snack.

1

Shrimp and Vegetables in Coconut Gravy *(Sayur Bobor)*

⅔ lb. (300g) spinach
½ chayote (Fig.1)
⅓ lb. (150g) shelled shrimp

1 ⎡ 3 shallots, sliced
     1 lemon grass, crushed
     1 T. ground fresh chilies
   ⎣ 1 t. shrimp paste (p.11)

2 ⎡ 1 c. ea.: stock, coconut milk

3 ⎡ ½ t. salt
   ⎣ 1 t. sugar

1 Cut spinach in sections and blanch in boiling water; remove. Cut chayote in pieces and boil 5 minutes, remove.

2 Combine ① and ②; bring to boil, reduce heat to low and cook 5 minutes until flavor is enhanced. Add ③, shrimp and cooked vegetables, bring to boil. Serve.

■ Goes well with rice, or can be poured on "compressed rice" (p.55), to which various kinds of spicy meat may be added to complete a well balanced meal. Add a little salt and oil to the water when cooking the vegetables to preserve the rich green colors.

印尼菜 Indonesian Cuisine   75

巴城牛肉粉絲湯

Batavia Beef Soup with Glass Noodles
(Soto Betawi)

< 4 人份 >

< SERVES 4 >

①	紅燒用瘦牛腿肉	12兩(450公克)	①	1 lb. (450g) beef (top round or London broil)	
	蔥蒜醬泥(見19頁)	4大匙		4 T. fragrant paste (p.19)	
	芫荽子粉、胡椒	各1小匙		1 t. ea.: coriander powder, pepper	
	肉桂(2.5公分)	1支		1 cinnamon stick, 1" (2.5cm)	
	豆蔻	½ 顆		½ nutmeg	
	法國香葉	4片		4 bay leaves	
	香茅(拍扁)	2支		2 lemon grass, crushed	
	南薑(拍扁)	4片		4 galangal slices, crushed	
	水或高湯	10杯		10 c. water or stock	
②	鹽、胡椒	各2小匙	②	2 t. ea.: salt, pepper	
	椰奶	2杯		2 c. coconut milk	
③	水煮蛋(切半)	2個	③	2 hard-boiled eggs, cut in half	
	青檸檬(切片)	4片		4 lime slices	
	番茄(直切成4塊)	2個		2 tomatoes, cut in quarters lengthwise	
	芹菜葉(略切)	¼ 杯		¼ c. celery leaves, coarsely cut	
	油蔥酥	2大匙		2 T. crispy shallots (p.15)	
	粉絲*(圖1)	4兩(150公克)		⅓ lb. (150g) glass noodles* (Fig.1)	
	綠豆芽	2杯		2 c. bean sprouts	

1 牛肉切塊以滾水川燙備用。

2 將①料加入牛肉塊燒開，改中火蓋鍋煮1½小時，至牛肉湯汁剩6杯，加入②料，再倒入椰奶燒開備用。

3 粉絲泡軟後連同豆芽分別以滾水川燙，若不馬上用，則以冷水略沖，瀝乾備用。

4 依序將豆芽、粉絲分盛於4個碗內，倒入滾燙之牛肉湯及牛肉塊，再依序加入③料。食時依喜好加"甜辣醬"(見17頁)。

* 粉絲乃綠豆粉製成的透明細條。使用前必須先泡水。

■ 習慣上最後會在湯內撒上"Emping"(類似炸薯片)若無則免用；此為非常受歡迎的印尼家鄉菜，可單吃或配飯當餐。

1 Cut beef into bite sizes, blanch in boiling water; set aside.

2 Add beef to ①; bring to boil. Reduce heat to medium, cover and cook 1½ hours. Remove beef and 6 c. of beef stock; add ② and coconut milk, bring to boil and set aside.

3 Soak glass noodles in water to soften; remove, drain and blanch. Separately, blanch bean sprouts. If not used immediately: rinse in cold water, drain and set aside.

4 Place equal portions of bean sprouts and glass noodles in 4 bowls, pour in beef and the soup equally to each bowl, then add ③ in the order listed. If desired, serve with "Sweet Sambal" (p.17).

* A transparent noodle made from mung bean powder. Soak in water prior to cooking.

■ Generally garnished with "Emping" (deep-fried melinjo nut chips), sprinkled on noodle soup. This is a traditional Indonesian family soup offering tasty flavors and delightful aromas. Often eaten with rice as a complete meal, or as a one dish meal.

1

椰汁牛肉丸子

< 4 人份 >

牛絞肉		12兩(450公克)
①	鹽	½ 小匙
	蛋	1個
	太白粉	1小匙
②	基本辣醬泥(見19頁)	4大匙
	蝦醬	1小匙
	南薑 2片，法國香葉 3片	
	番茄(切丁)	1個
③	椰奶	2杯
	鹽	½ 小匙
	辣椒絲、油蔥酥	各1大匙

1. 絞肉與①料混合攪拌均勻，搓成20個小丸子，以大火蒸10分鐘取出。

2. 油2大匙燒熱炒香②料，加入番茄丁炒至軟，隨入肉丸子及③料，燒開後改中火續煮5分鐘，起鍋前加入辣椒絲，盛起再撒上油蔥酥即可。

Beef Balls in Spicy Coconut Milk
(Sambal Goreng Printil)

< SERVES 4 >

1 lb. (450g) ground beef	
① ½ t. salt	
1 egg	
1 t. cornstarch	
② 4 T. basic chili paste (p.19)	
1 t. shrimp paste (p.11)	
2 galangal slices, 3 bay leaves	
1 tomato, diced	
③ 2 c. coconut milk	
½ t. salt	
1 T. ea.: shredded chili peppers, crispy shallots (p.15)	

1. Mix beef and ① and form into 20 small balls. Steam 10 minutes over high heat and remove.

2. Heat 2 T. oil; stir-fry ② until aromatic. Add tomato and stir-fry until soft. Add meat balls and ③; bring to boil, reduce heat to medium and cook 5 minutes. Add chili peppers and sprinkle on crispy shallots. Serve.

辣味牛肉片

< 4 人份 >

紅燒用牛瘦腿肉		1斤(600公克)
①	香茅(拍扁)	1支
	南薑、檸檬葉	各3片
	水 5杯， 鹽 1小匙	
	炸油	2杯
②	基本辣醬泥(見19頁)	8大匙
	鹽	1小匙
	糖、酸子汁	各1大匙

1. 整塊牛肉放入①料內燒開，改中火蓋鍋燜煮1小時，牛肉勿煮太爛撈出待涼，切半公分厚大薄片，並以刀背將肉片拍鬆，湯汁留做其他用途。

2. 炸油燒熱，大火將牛肉片炸1分鐘，顏色變深即可撈出。

3. 油4大匙燒熱，將②料依序炒香，再放入炸好的牛肉片拌炒均勻即可。

■ 這是一直被原住民喜愛的菜餚，適與"辣味全蛋"(見73頁)及"香草椰汁飯"(見73頁)一起食用。

Sliced Beef with Red Chili Sauce
(Sambal Daging)

< SERVES 4 >

1⅓ lbs. (600g) beef (top round or London broil)	
① 1 lemon grass, crushed	
3 ea.: galangal slices, kaffir leaves	
5 c. water, 1 t. salt	
2 c. oil for deep-frying	
② 8 T. basic chili paste (p.19)	
1 t. salt	
1 T. ea.: sugar, tamarind juice	

1. Place beef in ①; bring to boil. Reduce heat to medium; cover and cook 1 hour. Do not overcook. Remove and let cool; reserve beef stock. Slice and tenderize beef.

2. Heat oil; deep-fry beef slices for 1 minute over high heat. Remove when color darkens.

3. Heat 4 T. oil; stir-fry ② until aromatic. Add in cooked beef slices; stir and mix well. Serve.

■ This is one of the favorite dishes for the aboriginal people of Indonesia. Usually eaten with "Eggs in Spicy Red Sauce" and "Fragrant Coconut Rice" (p.73).

巴東辣牛肉

< 4 人份 >

紅燒用牛瘦腿肉 1斤（600公克）

①	臘仁辣醬泥（見19頁）	5大匙
	南薑泥	1大匙
	薑泥	1小匙
	香茅（拍扁）	1支
	檸檬葉	6片
	椰奶	2杯
②	鹽	1½ 小匙
	糖、酸子汁	各1小匙

1　牛肉切塊。

2　將①及②料混合以大火燒開，
加入牛肉再燒開，改小火蓋鍋
煮2小時至牛肉熟軟，續翻炒
至汁收乾出油為止。若牛肉已
熟爛而汁未收乾，可先取出牛
肉將汁煮略乾，再將牛肉回鍋
炒拌均勻。

■　此道菜起源於西蘇門答臘巴東
市，馳名於全印尼、馬來西
亞、和星加坡等地方。

香炒椰絲牛肉片

< 4 人份 >

牛排肉*（切薄片）		6兩（225公克）
椰茸		6兩（225公克）
①	椰子糖（搗碎）	2大匙
	紅蔥頭泥	2大匙
	蒜泥	1小匙
	芫荽子粉、酸子汁	各1大匙
	鹽	½ 小匙
	法國香葉	2片
	濃椰奶	¼ 杯

1　將①料混合以小火煮至糖溶
化，熄火立即取出。一半與牛
肉片混合拌勻，另一半與椰茸
拌勻。

2　鍋不放油，將牛肉片以小火炒
10分鐘，肉熟汁略收乾，再加
椰茸炒15分鐘至乾香為止。椰
茸容易炒焦，炒拌時必須用小
火不斷的翻拌。可與白飯、椰
汁香飯（見49頁）或飯糰（見55
頁）等配食。

*　除牛肉外也適用於豬肉。

■　在印尼此道菜非常的普遍；一
次多做些，放入玻璃罐內蓋
緊，可冷藏保存數星期。

Padang Style Spicy Beef *(Rendang Daging)*

1⅓ lbs. (600g) beef (top round
or London broil)

①
- 5 T. candlenut chili paste (p.19)
- 1 T. ground fresh galangal
- 1 t. ground ginger root
- 1 lemon grass, crushed
- 6 kaffir leaves
- 2 c. coconut milk

②
- 1½ t. salt
- 1 t. ea: sugar, tamarind juice

1 Cut beef into bite size pieces.

2 Mix ① and ② and bring to boil over high heat; add beef, and bring to boil again. Reduce heat to low; cover and cook for 2 hours until beef is tender. Continually stir-fry beef until sauce is absorbed. If there is too much sauce, remove beef and continue to cook sauce until most of it evaporates, return meat to sauce and stir-fry briefly.

■ This dish originated in the city of Padang located on the Western side of the Island of Sumatra. Because of its popularity, it can be found throughout Indonesia, Malaysia and Singapore.

Fried Grated Coconut With Beef *(Serundeng Daging)*

½ lb. (225g) beef* (sliced
top sirloin)

½ lb. (225g) shredded
coconut

①
- 2 T. palm sugar (crushed)
- 2 T. ground shallots
- 1 t. ground fresh garlic
- 1 T. coriander powder
- 1 T. tamarind juice
- ½ t. salt
- 2 bay leaves
- ¼ c. thick coconut milk

1 Mix ①; cook over low heat until sugar melts; turn off heat and remove immediately. Mix half of the mixture ① with the beef and the other half with shredded coconut.

2 Place beef in a dry pan and stir-fry over low heat for 10 minutes until cooked and sauce is almost absorbed. Add in the shredded coconut; stir 15 minutes until dry and aromatic. Low heat and continuous stirring is essential to avoid burning the coconut. Serve with rice, "Coconut Rice" (p.49) or "Compressed Rice" (p.55).

* May substitute pork for beef.

■ This dish goes best with rice. A large amount can be prepared and stored in tightly sealed jar(s) and preserved for many weeks in a refrigerator.

黃薑炸雞

< 2 人份 >

	帶骨雞或雞腿	1斤(600公克)
①	鹽 ½ 小匙，青檸檬汁	1小匙
	蔥蒜醬泥(見19頁)	4大匙
	芫荽子粉	1大匙
	黃薑粉	½ 小匙
②	南薑泥	2大匙
	法國香葉	2片
	香茅(拍扁)	1支
	鹽 ½ 小匙，糖 1小匙	
	炸油	2杯

1 雞切塊以①料醃1小時，再入②料拌勻，倒入不沾鍋，蓋鍋以小火燜20分鐘至熟中途再翻拌，若剩很多湯汁，則需用大火將汁收乾。

2 炸油燒熱，中火將雞塊炸4分鐘至金黃色，撈出盛在盤上，油內的香料渣子也可撈起瀝乾，撒在雞塊上。配"蝦醬味辣醬"(見16頁)食用。

■ 在印尼有"黃薑炸雞"的專賣店，可見其知名度，在家若不喜食油炸，則僅做到作法1即可。

Fragrant Fried Turmeric Chicken
(Ayam Goreng Kuning)

< SERVES 2 >

	1⅓ lbs. (600g) chicken with bones or chicken legs	
①	½ t. salt, 1 t. lime juice	
	4 T. fragrant paste (p.19)	
	1 T. coriander powder	
	½ t. turmeric powder	
②	2 T. ground fresh galangal	
	2 bay leaves	
	1 lemon grass, crushed	
	½ t. salt, 1 t. sugar	
	2 c. oil for deep-frying	

1 Cut chicken to bite size pieces; Rub with ①; let stand for 1 hour. Mix with ②, place in a non-stick pan; cover and cook over low heat 20 minutes until just cooked, turning occasionally. If sauce remains, turn heat to high and cook until evaporated.

2 Heat oil; fry chicken over medium heat for 4 minutes until golden brown, remove to a plate. Collect leftovers of ② from oil and sprinkle on chicken. Serve with "Shrimp Paste Sambal" (p.16).

■ If you prefer non-deep-fried chicken, omit procedure 2. There are many stores that specialize in selling this dish in Indonesia.

白汁燜雞

< 2 人份 >

	帶骨雞或雞腿	1斤(600公克)
①	鹽、胡椒	各½ 小匙
	蔥蒜醬泥(見19頁)	4大匙
	芫荽子粉、胡椒	各1大匙
②	香茅(拍扁)	1支
	法國香葉、南薑	各3片
	高湯	1杯
③	濃椰奶	½ 杯
	鹽 ½ 小匙，糖 1小匙	
	油蔥酥	1大匙

1 雞切塊以①料醃30分鐘，用5大匙油煎至表面呈金黃色。

2 隨加②料煮開，蓋鍋以小火煮20分鐘至肉熟，續入③料，大火煮至汁變濃，撒上油蔥酥，亦可隨喜好撒上辣椒絲。

Braised Chicken in White Gravy
(Opor Ayam)

< SERVES 2 >

	1⅓ lbs. (600g) chicken with bones or chicken legs	
①	½ t. ea.: salt, pepper	
	4 T. fragrant paste (p.19)	
	1 T. ea.: coriander powder, pepper	
②	1 lemon grass, crushed	
	3 ea.: bay leaves, galangal slices	
	1 c. stock	
③	½ c. thick coconut milk	
	½ t. salt, 1 t. sugar	
	1 T. crispy shallots (p.15)	

1 Cut chicken to bite size pieces; Rub with ①; let stand for 30 minutes. Pan-fry chicken in 5 T. oil until golden brown.

2 Add in ②; bring to boil. Reduce heat to low; cover and cook 20 minutes. Add ③, turn heat to high, cook until sauce thickens. Sprinkle on crispy shallots, or shredded chili peppers if preferred. Serve with rice.

辣醬烤雞

Grilled Chicken with Red Hot Sauce
(Ayam Pangang Bumbu Merah)

< 4 人份 >　　　　　< SERVES 4 >

雞	2斤4兩(1350公克)	3 lbs. (1350g) chicken	
① 鹽	1小匙	① 1 t. salt	
青檸檬汁	1大匙	1 T. lime juice	
② 基本辣醬泥(見19頁)	6大匙	② 6 T. basic chili paste (p.19)	
香茅(拍扁)	2支	2 lemon grass, crushed	
③ 鹽	½ 小匙	③ ½ t. salt	
糖	1小匙	1 t. sugar	
酸子汁	1大匙	1 T. tamarind juice	

1　雞從胸部直切開，以刀背敲壓骨頭，將雞壓扁呈蝴蝶狀，以①料醃1小時，烤箱預熱220℃(425°F)，將雞皮朝上烤30分鐘。

2　油3大匙燒熱，炒香②料，加入③料炒勻鏟出，醬汁塗抹在雞表面。

3　烤箱再燒熱，260℃(500°F)將雞用上火烤10分鐘至表面呈金黃色即可。

■　此道菜色香味俱全，又可事先準備，是一道方便的宴客菜餚。

1　Cut chicken down the breast, open up and crush the spine; open to butterfly the chicken. Cover with ①; let stand for 1 hour. Preheat oven to 425°F(220℃); place in oven, skin side up, and bake 30 minutes.

2　Heat 3 T. oil; stir-fry ② until aromatic. Add ③, stir and mix well, remove and coat chicken.

3　Heat oven to 500°F(260℃) and bake 10 minutes until golden brown. Remove and garnish with lettuce. Serve.

■　This dish combines the aroma, flavor and colors of the most desirable of Indonesian cuisine. Can be conveniently prepared in advance.

爪哇炸豆腐

Javanese Spicy Tofu *(Tahu Gejrot)*

< 4 人份 >　　　　　< SERVES 4 >

老豆腐	12兩(450公克)	1 lb. (450g) firm tofu	
炸油	2杯	2 c. oil for deep-frying	
① 基本辣醬泥(見19頁)	1½ 大匙	① 1½ T. basic chili paste (p.19)	
水	¼ 杯	¼ c. water	
酸子汁、青檸檬汁、糖	各1大匙	1 T. ea.: tamarind juice, lime juice, sugar	
甜醬油	4大匙	4 T. sweet soy sauce	

1　豆腐切成16塊。炸油燒熱將豆腐以大火炸5分鐘至表面呈金黃色。

2　將①料混合以中火燒開，改小火煮5分鐘，淋在豆腐上面。

■　帶有甜酸辣味的炸豆腐，可當前菜或配飯菜，開胃可口。

1　Cut tofu into 16 pieces; heat oil and deep-fry tofu over high heat for 5 minutes until golden brown.

2　Mix ①; bring to boil over medium heat. Reduce heat to low and cook 5 minutes and pour over tofu.

■　Makes an excellent appetizer or main dish because of the sweet, sour, and spicy flavor.

香蕉葉烤魚

<　2 人 份　>

魚		1斤(600公克)
①	基本辣醬泥(見19頁)	5大匙
	蝦醬	1小匙
	鹽	1¼ 小匙
	糖	1½ 小匙
	青檸檬汁	1大匙
	檸檬葉(切絲)	1大匙
	香茅(切片)	1大匙
香蕉葉		1大片

1　魚肉厚處劃刀痕，以①料醃1小時。

2　在香蕉葉表面擦上1大匙油，將魚置上將魚包捲好，兩端以竹籤固定。

3　烤箱預熱200℃(400℉)，放入魚烤25分鐘即成。依個人喜好，可淋數滴青檸檬汁。

■　印尼當地盛產香蕉，利用香蕉葉烤出來的菜餚別具香味，也呈現出傳統特色。

甜汁烤魚

<　2 人 份　>

魚		1斤(600公克)
①	鹽、青檸檬汁	各1小匙
②	基本辣醬泥(見19頁)	2大匙
	薑泥	1小匙
	甜醬油	3大匙
	醬油	½ 大匙
	番茄醬	1大匙
炸油		2杯

1　在魚肉厚處劃刀痕，以①料醃30分鐘，拭乾水份。

2　炸油燒熱，將魚大火炸5分鐘、至表面呈金黃色撈出，隨即塗抹拌勻的②料，置烤盤上。

3　烤箱預熱200℃(400℉)，放入魚烤5分鐘至醬汁乾香(若用烤架，每面烤5分鐘)。可隨喜愛與“蝦醬味辣醬”(見16頁)沾食。

■　不喜歡油炸者，可直接塗抹①、②料，用烤箱200℃(400℉)烤20分鐘。此道菜味香濃，與生菜、黃瓜配食即成豐盛正餐。

Spicy Fish Baked in Banana Leaves *(Pepes Ikan Bumbu Merah)*

< SERVES 2 >

1⅓ lbs. (600g) fish

① ⎡ 5 T. basic chili paste (p.19)
  │ 1 t. shrimp paste (p.11)
  │ 1¼ t. salt
  │ 1½ t. sugar
  │ 1 T. ea.: lime juice, shredded
  │   kaffir leaves
  ⎣ 1 T. lemon grass, sliced

1 large banana leaf

1   Make crisscross cuts on the thick part of the fish. Marinate in ① for 1 hour.

2   Coat banana leaf with 1 T. oil; place fish on leaf. Roll up fish in the leaf and skewer it with toothpicks to hold each end closed.

3   Preheat oven to 400°F(200°C) and bake fish for 25 minutes; serve. Drip on lime juice, if desired.

■ Because of the abundance of bananas in Indonesia, the use of their leaves in baking is the traditional baking method. This creates the distinctive exotic flavors enjoyed by all.

Grilled Fish with Sweet Soy Sauce *(Ikan Bakar Kecap Manis)*

< SERVES 2 >

1⅓ lbs. (600g) fish

① ⎡ 1 t. ea.: salt, lime juice

② ⎡ 2 T. basic chili paste (p.19)
  │ 1 t. ground ginger root
  │ 3 T. sweet soy sauce
  │ ½ T. soy sauce
  ⎣ 1 T. ketchup

2 c. oil for deep-frying

1   Make crisscross cuts across the thick part of the fish; rub with ①; let stand for 30 minutes. Pat dry.

2   Heat oil; deep-fry fish over high heat for 5 minutes until golden brown; remove immediately and coat with mixture ②; place in a baking pan.

3   Preheat oven to 400°F(200°C); bake fish 5 minutes until sauce is evaporated and aromatic. If cooked on a barbeque grill, grill fish 5 minutes on each side. Serve with "Shrimp Paste Sambal" (p.16).

■ If deep-frying is not preferred, coat fish with ① and ② then bake in an oven for 20 minutes at 400°F(200°C) to achieve similar delicious results. This dish has a pleasant aroma. It can be served with cucumbers and lettuce as a complete main dish.

茄汁魷魚

< 4 人份 >

魷魚	12兩 (450公克)
① 鹽 ½ 小匙，糖 2大匙	
酸子汁	1大匙
紅蔥頭泥	2大匙
蒜泥	1小匙
番茄醬	5大匙

1 魷魚洗淨瀝乾水份，將頭塞進肚內，以牙籤封口 (圖1)，以①料醃過夜。

2 油6大匙燒熱，將魷魚連同醃汁一起放入，以大火煮約5分鐘至魷魚熟，汁略收乾。可與黃瓜及番茄片配食。

■ 這種加了番茄醬帶有酸甜的味道，是受荷蘭飲食文化的影響。若無新鮮魷魚冷凍的亦可 (圖2)。

峇里辣醬炸魚

< 4 人份 >

魚排	12兩 (450公克)
① 鹽、青檸檬汁	各1小匙
炸油	2杯
② 臘仁辣醬泥 (見19頁)	5大匙
薑泥	1小匙
鹽	¼ 小匙
③ 甜醬油	1½ 大匙
酸子汁	1小匙

1 魚洗淨拭乾，以①料醃30分鐘。

2 炸油燒熱，將魚大火炸6分鐘至剛熟表面呈金黃色。

3 油3大匙燒熱，炒香②料隨即加③料略炒，再將炸好的魚放入翻拌均勻即成。

■ 這種帶有甜酸辣味的作法，是印尼很普遍的配飯菜餚，魚排或全魚可任選。

Squid with Spicy Tomato Sauce
(Sotong Goreng Saus Tomat)

< SERVES 4 >

1 lb. (450g) squid	
½ t. salt , 2 T. sugar	
1 T. tamarind juice	
① 2 T. ground shallots	
1 t. ground fresh garlic	
5 T. ketchup	

1 Wash squid and drain. Push the squid head into its stomach and close the opening with toothpicks (Fig.1). Cover with ① overnight.

2 Heat 6 T. oil; add squid and marinade and cook 5 minutes over high heat until sauce thickens. Serve with cucumber and tomato slices.

■ The addition of the ketchup in this dish enhances the sweet and sour flavor and is the result of the influence of the Dutch culture. Frozen squid (Fig.2) may be used as a substitute for fresh squid.

Balinese Fried Fish *(Ikan Bumbu Bali)*

< SERVES 4 >

1 lb. (450g) fish fillet	
① 1 t. ea.: salt, lime juice	
2 c. oil for deep-frying	
② 5 T. candlenut chili paste (p.19)	
1 t. ground ginger root	
¼ t. salt	
③ 1½ T. sweet soy sauce	
1 t. tamarind juice	

1 Clean fish and pat dry; Rub with ①; let stand for 30 minutes.

2 Heat oil; deep-fry fish over high heat for 6 minutes until just cooked and golden brown.

3 Heat 3 T. oil; stir-fry ② until aromatic, add ③, and stir lightly. Add fish and mix well, serve.

■ The special way the sweet, sour and spicy flavors are combined in the cooking method, makes this a very popular favorite in Indonesia. May use the whole fish as well as the fish fillet.

1

2

烤大頭蝦

Indonesian Barbequed Prawns
(Bakar Udang Gala)

<　2 人 份　>

<　SERVES 2　>

大頭蝦	12兩(450公克)
鹽	½ 小匙
甜醬油	2大匙
① 酸子汁	1大匙
蒜頭汁、辣椒泥	各1小匙
油	1大匙

1 lb. (450g) fresh water prawns	
½ t. salt	
2 T. sweet soy sauce	
① 1 T. tamarind juice	
1 t. ea.: garlic juice, ground fresh chili	
1 T. oil	

1　蝦去腸泥洗淨瀝乾，將每隻蝦由背部直切開，以①料醃過夜。

2　烤架預熱200℃(400°F)，每面各烤3分鐘。

■　若用炭火燒烤，以醃蝦餘汁邊塗邊烤風味更佳，在雅加達許多夜市的路邊攤就因燒烤的香味吸引了不少食客。

1　Devein prawns; wash and drain. Lengthwise, cut through along the outer curve of each prawn. Marinate in ① overnight.

2　Preheat electric grill to 400°F (200℃), bake each side for 3 minutes. Serve.

■　When barbequing, brush on ① while cooking. This enhances the natural flavors of this dish. In addition, the aroma attracts the Indonesian people who enjoy the food stands and night markets located throughout Jakarta and other cities.

炸大頭蝦

Fried Prawns with Dipping Sauce
(Goreng Udang Gala)

<　2 人 份　>

<　SERVES 2　>

大頭蝦	12兩(450公克)
① 鹽、胡椒	各1小匙
炸油	2杯
碎花生(見15頁)、辣椒泥	各1大匙
番茄醬	1大匙
② 紅蔥頭(切薄片)	1粒
青檸檬汁、甜醬油	各1大匙
紅辣椒(略切)	1小匙

1 lb. (450g) fresh water prawns	
① 1 t. ea.: salt, pepper	
2 c. oil for deep-frying	
1 T. ea.: ground peanuts (p.15), ground fresh chilies	
1 T. ketchup	
② 1 shallot, sliced	
1 T. ea.: lime juice, sweet soy sauce	
1 t. red chili peppers, coarsely cut	

1　蝦去腸泥洗淨瀝乾，以①料醃1小時。

2　炸油燒熱，將蝦炸1至2分鐘至蝦肉熟，表面呈金黃色，沾拌勻的②料食用。

■　印尼本地盛產大頭蝦，大頭蝦料理樣式多且廣受喜愛，這種外殼酥脆，蝦肉鮮嫩的作法是先母常做的一道菜。

1　Devein prawns; wash and drain. Coat with ①; let stand for 1 hour.

2　Heat oil; deep-fry prawns 1 to 2 minutes until cooked and golden brown. Serve with mixture ②.

■　Fresh water prawns can be found all over Indonesia and are a popular staple in many dishes. This method was often used by my mother and results in a very crispy outside while providing a very tender inside.

酪梨奶冰

< 2 人 份 >

酪梨(圖1)	1個
① 糖	¼ 杯
煉奶	2大匙
青檸檬汁	½ 大匙
冰塊	1½ 杯

1 酪梨去皮切塊

2 將酪梨塊及①料放入攪碎機內，攪細即成。

■ 此種冰點像霜淇淋，是荷蘭飲食文化的流傳。喜愛巧克力者，可加點巧克力糖漿。

炸香蕉

< 1 6 個 >

香蕉	4條
① 粘米粉，麵粉	各½ 杯
鹽	¼ 小匙
香草精	½ 小匙
水	⅔ 杯
炸油	2杯

1 每條香蕉切成4片(圖2)。

2 將①料混合，加水攪拌成麵糊。

3 炸油2杯燒熱，將香蕉沾裹麵糊，中火炸3分鐘至表面呈金黃色即成。

■ 粘米粉即米磨成粉。拌好的麵糊可用來炸不同蔬果，在印尼各地的夜市，人人都會買些炸香蕉，邊逛邊吃，這是當地便宜又好吃的零食。

黑糯米甜粥

< 4 人 份 >

黑、白糯米*	各 ⅔ 杯	② 鹽	¼ 小匙
① 椰子糖	8兩(300公克)	濃椰奶	1杯
水	8杯		
香蘭葉	3片		

1 糯米洗淨後與①料一起燒開，改小火蓋鍋煮2小時(煮時宜用不沾鍋，以免黏鍋)，中途需攪拌成糯米粥，隨即分盛4碗。

2 將②料以微波爐加熱30秒，見表面起小泡泡立即取出，分別淋在粥內。

* 糯米有黑及白二種，內含豐富的澱粉質，味香甜口感佳。

■ 此為星馬印非常流行的甜粥，居家常備這種甜粥，做為小孩放學後的點心。

Avocado Milkshake *(Es Apokat)*

1 avocado (Fig.1)

① ¼ c. sugar
2 T. condensed milk
½ T. lime juice
1½ c. ice cubes

1 Remove skin of avocado; cut it to bite-size pieces.

2 Place ① and avocado in blender; blend to fine. Serve.

■ This deliciously exotic, thick dessert has the same consistency as a milkshake and originated with the Dutch culture. Should a "chocolate" flavor be desired, a small amount of chocolate syrup may be added.

Fried Banana *(Pisang Goreng)*

4 bananas

① ½ c. rice flour
½ c. all purpose flour
¼ t. salt
½ t. vanilla extract
⅔ c. water
2 c. oil for deep-frying

1 Slice each banana to 4 pieces (Fig.2).

2 Mix ①; add water, stir to make a smooth batter.

3 Heat oil; dip the pieces of banana in the batter; remove banana and deep-fry over medium heat for 3 minutes until golden brown. Serve.

■ Rice flour is available in Asian markets. Other kinds of fruit or vegetables may be deep-fried in the rice batter, if desired. This is a popular snack throughout Indonesia often enjoyed between meals.

2

Black Sticky Rice in Sweet Coconut Milk *(Bubur Ketan Hitam)*

⅔ c. black glutinous rice
⅔ c. glutinous rice*

① ⅔ lb. (300g) palm sugar
8 c. water
3 pandan leaves

② ¼ t. salt
1 c. thick coconut milk

1 Wash rice; mix with ① and bring to boil. Reduce heat to low, cover and cook for 2 hours, stirring occasionally. It is best to use a non-stick pan. Place equal portions in 4 bowls.

2 Mix ② and heat in microwave for 30 seconds. Remove when simmering, pour on top of rice.

* Glutinous rice contains high levels of starch, offering a sweeter taste than regular rice.

■ A very popular traditional family dessert in Singapore, Malaysia and Indonesia, often served to the children after school.

索 引

INDEX

MORE FROM WEI-CHUAN PUBLISHING

• ALL COOKBOOKS ARE BILINGUAL (ENGLISH/CHINESE) UNLESS FOOTNOTED OTHERWISE •

CHINESE CUISINE
APPETIZERS, CHINESE STYLE
CHINESE COOKING MADE EASY
CHINESE CUISINE
CHINESE COOKING FAVORITE HOME DISHES
CHINESE COOKING FOR BEGINNERS [1]
FAVORITE CHINESE DISHES
FISH, CHINESE STYLE MADE EASY [3]
SHELLFISH, CHINESE STYLE MADE EASY [3]

CHINESE REGIONAL CUISINE
CHINESE CUISINE, BEIJING STYLE
CHINESE CUISINE, CANTONESE STYLE
CHINESE CUISINE, SHANGHAI STYLE
CHINESE CUISINE, SZECHWAN STYLE
CHINESE CUISINE, TAIWANESE STYLE

GARNISHES
CHINESE APPETIZERS & GARNISHES
GREAT GARNISHES

HEALTHFUL COOKING
CHINESE HERB COOKING FOR HEALTH
CHINESE HOME COOKING FOR HEALTH
HEALTHFUL COOKING
LOW-CHOLESTEROL CHINESE CUISINE
SIMPLY VEGETARIAN
VEGETARIAN COOKING

INTERNATIONAL CUISINE
INDIAN CUISINE
JAPANESE CUISINE
KOREAN CUISINE
MEXICAN COOKING MADE EASY [4]

ONE DISH MEALS FROM POPULAR CUISINES [3]
SINGAPOREAN, MALAYSIAN, & INDONESIAN CUISINE
THAI COOKING MADE EASY
VIETNAMESE CUISINE

RICE & NOODLES
NOODLES, CHINESE HOME-COOKING
NOODLES, CLASSICAL CHINESE COOKING
RICE, CHINESE HOME-COOKING
RICE, TRADITIONAL CHINESE COOKING

SPECIALTIES
CHINESE DIM SUM
CHINESE SNACKS, REVISED
CREATIVE CHINESE OVEN COOKING
INTERNATIONAL BAKING DELIGHTS

COMPACT COOKBOOK SERIES
BEEF [2]
CHICKEN
SOUP! SOUP! SOUP!
TOFU! TOFU! TOFU!
VEGETABLES [2]
VERY! VERY! VEGETARIAN!

VIDEOS
CHINESE GARNISHES I [5]
CHINESE GARNISHES II [5]
CHINESE STIR-FRYING: BEEF [5]
CHINESE STIR-FRYING: CHICKEN [5]
CHINESE STIR-FRYING: VEGETABLES [5]

OTHERS
CARVING TOOLS

FOOTNOTES

1. Also available in English/Spanish, French/Chinese, and German/Chinese   **2**. English and Chinese are in separate editions
3. Trilingual English/Chinese/Spanish edition   **4**. Also available in English/Spanish   **5**. English Only

Wei-Chuan Cookbooks can be purchased in the U.S.A., Canada and twenty other countries worldwide
1455 Monterey Pass Road, #110, Monterey Park, CA 91754, U.S.A. • Tel: (323)261-3880 • Fax: (323) 261-3299

∎

味全叢書

中國菜系列	省份菜	拼盤·米·麵	健康系列	點心·烘焙·燒烤	異國風味	小食譜
中國菜	上海菜	拼盤與盤飾	養生藥膳	點心專輯	南洋菜	豆腐
速簡中國菜	四川菜	盤飾精選	養生家常菜	飲茶食譜	泰國菜	湯
實用中國菜 [1]	北京菜	米食，家常篇	健康食譜	實用烘焙	越南菜	家庭素食
實用家庭菜	台灣菜	米食，傳統篇	均衡飲食	創意燒烤	印度菜	牛肉 [2]
美味小菜	廣東菜	麵，家常篇	健康素		韓國菜	雞肉 [2]
魚 [3]		麵，精華篇	素食		日本料理	疏菜 [2]
家常100					墨西哥菜 [4]	
蝦、貝、蟹 [3]					簡餐（五國風味）[3]	

(如無數字標註，即為中英對照版)

1 中英、英西、中法、中德版   **2** 中文版及英文版   **3** 中英西對照版   **4** 中英版及英西版

味全食譜在台、美加及全球二十餘國皆有發行・味全出版社有限公司・台北市仁愛路4段28號2樓
Tel: (02) 2702-1148   ・   Fax: (02) 2704-2729

∎

OTROS LIBROS DE WEI-CHUAN
EDICIONES EN ESPAÑOL

Cocina China Para Principiantes, Edición Revisada [1]
Cocina Popular de Un Solo Platillo [2]
Comida Mexicana, Fácil de Preparar [3]
Mariscos, Estilo Chino Fácil de Preparar [2]
Pescado, Estilo Chino Fácil de Preparar [2]

---

1 Disponible en Inglés/Español, Inglés/Chino, Francés/Chino, y Alemán/Chino
2 Edición trilingüe Inglés/Chino/Español
3 Disponible en ediciones bilingües Inglés/Español e Inglés/Chino

Los Libros de Cocina Wei-Chuan se pueden comprar en E.E.U.U., Canadá y otros 20 países a través del mundo.